# THE BIG BANG PROJECT

# THE BIG BANG PROJECT
## CREATING HUMANITY'S BEST-CASE SCENARIO

LUC GOULET

TRUE DIRECTIONS
AN AFFILIATE OF TARCHER BOOKS

iUniverse®

# THE BIG BANG PROJECT
## CREATING HUMANITY'S BEST-CASE SCENARIO

*iUniverse books may be ordered through booksellers or by contacting:*

*iUniverse*
*1663 Liberty Drive*
*Bloomington, IN 474037*
*www.iuniverse.com*
*1-800-Authors (1-800-288-4677)*

*Because of the dynamic nature of the Internet, any web addresses or links contained in this book may have changed since publication and may no longer be valid. The views expressed in this work are solely those of the author and do not necessarily reflect the views of the publisher, and the publisher hereby disclaims any responsibility for them.*

*Any people depicted in stock imagery provided by Thinkstock are models, and such images are being used for illustrative purposes only.*
*Certain stock imagery © Thinkstock.*

*ISBN: 978-1-4917-6443-5 (sc)*
*ISBN: 978-1-4917-6444-2 (hc)*
*ISBN: 978-1-4917-6445-9 (e)*

*Library of Congress Control Number: 2015904959*

*Print information available on the last page.*

*iUniverse rev. date: 5/6/2015*

# CONTENTS

Acknowledgments . . . . . . . . . . . . . . . . . . . . . . . . . . . . . . . . . . . . . . . . . ix

Author's Note . . . . . . . . . . . . . . . . . . . . . . . . . . . . . . . . . . . . . . . . . . . . xi

**INTRODUCTION** . . . . . . . . . . . . . . . . . . . . . . . . . . . . . . . . . . . . . . . . . . . . **XV**

    The Vision . . . . . . . . . . . . . . . . . . . . . . . . . . . . . . . . . . . . . . . . . . . . . xvi

    The Mission . . . . . . . . . . . . . . . . . . . . . . . . . . . . . . . . . . . . . . . . . . . .xvii

**1   HUMAN EVOLUTION: CAN WE DO BETTER?** . . . . . . . . . . . . . . . . . . . . . . . . .1

**2   PREMISES FOR A POSITIVE EVOLUTION** . . . . . . . . . . . . . . . . . . . . . . . . . . .5

    The Humble Human Perspective . . . . . . . . . . . . . . . . . . . . . . . . . . .7

**3   A BETTER ME, A BETTER WE—AND VICE VERSA** . . . . . . . . . . . . . . . . . . . .11

    What Comes after the "Me, Myself, and I" Era? . . . . . . . . . . . . .11

    The Great Power of Giving . . . . . . . . . . . . . . . . . . . . . . . . . . . . .12

    One Platform—All the Options. . . . . . . . . . . . . . . . . . . . . . . . . .16

    Idea for a Super Reality TV Show . . . . . . . . . . . . . . . . . . . . . . .18

    Education versus Knowledge . . . . . . . . . . . . . . . . . . . . . . . . . . .19

**4   SHOULD GOVERNMENTS AND DEMOCRACY EVOLVE?** . . . . . . . . . . . . . . . . .23

    Management. . . . . . . . . . . . . . . . . . . . . . . . . . . . . . . . . . . . . . . . .28

    Competence. . . . . . . . . . . . . . . . . . . . . . . . . . . . . . . . . . . . . . . . .29

    Transparency, Accountability, and a Strict Code of Ethics . . . . .29

    Responsibilities . . . . . . . . . . . . . . . . . . . . . . . . . . . . . . . . . . . . . .30

    Political Parties and Independents . . . . . . . . . . . . . . . . . . . . . . .31

Neutrality . . . . . . . . . . . . . . . . . . . . . . . . . . . . . . . . . . . . . .33
Party Funding and Advertising. . . . . . . . . . . . . . . . . . . . . . . .33
The Voting System. . . . . . . . . . . . . . . . . . . . . . . . . . . . . . . .35
Electoral Process . . . . . . . . . . . . . . . . . . . . . . . . . . . . . . . . .35
Up-to-Date Technology. . . . . . . . . . . . . . . . . . . . . . . . . . . . .35
Voting for the Right Reasons . . . . . . . . . . . . . . . . . . . . . . . .36
Voting for Important Issues . . . . . . . . . . . . . . . . . . . . . . . . .37
A Proper Majority . . . . . . . . . . . . . . . . . . . . . . . . . . . . . . . .37
International Interventions. . . . . . . . . . . . . . . . . . . . . . . . . .39

5   CAN GOVERNMENTS PLAY A BETTER ROLE TO IMPROVE ECONOMIES? . . . . . . .43
A National Debt for Legacy? . . . . . . . . . . . . . . . . . . . . . . . . .44
Performance Indicators. . . . . . . . . . . . . . . . . . . . . . . . . . . . .47
Evaluate Public Services and Cost Sharing . . . . . . . . . . . . . . .50
Every Dollar Counts . . . . . . . . . . . . . . . . . . . . . . . . . . . . . . .51
Day care and Kindergarten. . . . . . . . . . . . . . . . . . . . . . . . . . .55
Primary School and High School . . . . . . . . . . . . . . . . . . . . . .56
College and University . . . . . . . . . . . . . . . . . . . . . . . . . . . . .56
Shared Costs for People with Special Health-Care Needs . . . . .59
Private Insurance for Surgery—More Personal Responsibility
for Regular Care . . . . . . . . . . . . . . . . . . . . . . . . . . . . . . . . . .59

6   CAPITALISM: IS THE RIGHT ON THE RIGHT COURSE? . . . . . . . . . . . . . . . . . . . . .63
The Game Changed, but Who Has the Advantage? . . . . . . . . . .64
Too Big to Fail Equals Too Big to Exist As Is? . . . . . . . . . . . . .65
The Right's Social Responsibilities. . . . . . . . . . . . . . . . . . . . . .68
Avoid the Void; There Are No Jobs There. . . . . . . . . . . . . . . . .69
Who Benefits the Most without the Responsibility? . . . . . . . . . .71
Evolving from "Win-Win" to "Win-Win-Win". . . . . . . . . . . . . .72

7   CAN CAPITALISM BE SAVED? . . . . . . . . . . . . . . . . . . . . . . . . . . . . . . . . . . . . . . .75
Rethinking Our Behaviors . . . . . . . . . . . . . . . . . . . . . . . . . . .75
The Great Cost of Savings . . . . . . . . . . . . . . . . . . . . . . . . . . .75
Buying Is Voting . . . . . . . . . . . . . . . . . . . . . . . . . . . . . . . . . .78
Can Labels Change Your Vote? . . . . . . . . . . . . . . . . . . . . . . . .80

The Best Models for Spreading Wealth . . . . . . . . . . . . . . . . . . .81

Technology and Service. . . . . . . . . . . . . . . . . . . . . . . . . . . . . . . .85

**8  THE BIG BANG PROJECT'S REVIEW AND ACTION PLAN. . . . . . . . . . . . . . . . . . . .87**

The Big Bang Project's Action Plan (Phase 1) . . . . . . . . . . . . . .89

**9  RELIGION—SADLY, AN IMPORTANT ISSUE. . . . . . . . . . . . . . . . . . . . . . . . . . . .91**

The Great Plan for Peace . . . . . . . . . . . . . . . . . . . . . . . . . . . . . .95

The Summit of All Summits. . . . . . . . . . . . . . . . . . . . . . . . . . . .95

Letter from Humanity to Religious Extremists. . . . . . . . . . . . .100

**CONCLUSION. . . . . . . . . . . . . . . . . . . . . . . . . . . . . . . . . . . . . . . . . . . . . . .105**

# ACKNOWLEDGMENTS

Many people have played very important roles in the creation of this book and project. You all have a special place in my heart. Thank you. My incredibly beautiful life partner, wife, and best friend (all in one), your precious devotion was key to realizing my dream. I will be eternally grateful. I love you and thank you for sharing my life. My boys have been quite patient through this long process. Thanks, guys. I love you so much. I wrote *The Big Bang Project* mostly for you.

My parents, brother, and sister made me a blessed man. I have such a great family that provided the perfect environment of love, respect, and building great things by working together. We use our differences to our advantage.

My teachers taught me so much. Thank you, Mr. Pollender, for sharing your passion for chess with me. It taught me to work with logic and imagination, and always try to predict a few moves ahead.

To my precious buddies, our conversations and arguments were a fantastic help. Thank you, Nathlou and Blou, for your peaceful home, the perfect place for inspiration, and breaking the "blank-page syndrome."

Eric, from "Descormiers et Associés", your contribution of examples of performance indicators is much appreciated. Véronique Hamel, I'm very grateful for your beautiful illustrations.

# AUTHOR'S NOTE

My ambitious goal is to trigger mankind's next phase of evolution. I believe that humans can evolve in a positive way. I spent the last thirty-five years asking myself how we can best progress as individuals, society, and species.

It all started with a commitment I made myself one sleepless night, at the age of fifteen, during the summer of 1979. I had just accomplished the improbable by getting rid of the heavy stutter I have had all my life, thanks to the practice of self-hypnosis. I had learned that I can reprogram myself—and that I can use this technique at will, for anything. I understood that there are no limits to our capabilities if we truly believe it and have a strong positive focus. I learned as well that for positive change to happen, you need to use positive suggestions and thoughts. That forces oneself to reinvent many new lines of questioning. Asking the right question in a positive manner can be transposed in everything you do. My first vision that night was that I would one day write a book to help people achieve the best they can be and to explain that anything we want to change, we can.

As I developed a national retail chain of franchised stores with my sister and brother, I kept my project on the back burner. Always adapting to new markets requires an open mind, research, and respect for different cultures. Managing a fast-growing company makes you great at understanding priorities, training, delegating, and motivating. In order to succeed, you understand that it can only be done by teamwork and that every member is important.

Throughout the years, these thoughts of sharing self-improvement methods evolved into social questioning and ideas about human evolution. Being an insomniac gave me lots of time to ask myself if there can be better ways for democracy to be expressed and whether capitalism can evolve in a positive manner to better create and spread wealth.

After selling my shares to my partner at the age of thirty-five, I devoted myself to my family and my passions while completing my MBA. Again, all those best principles of management may be used in many other spheres of our lives, personal and social.

I then experienced how volunteering helps others and is an important aspect of becoming a better human being. After a few years, I decided to go ahead with my lifelong mission. All my life's experiences made me feel confident and ready to share my vision for humanity's best path of evolution.

I am not a politician, and I do not represent any private organization or religious group. I'm not a specialist; I'm a generalist, someone with a global view.

Bono sings "One Voice," inspiring us to speak out. That's what I'm doing. I'm simply the voice of a fellow earthling, guided by a genuine love and respect for people, imagination, and common sense, with an extraordinary vision of a better world.

Instead of going into great details, I chose to treat more concepts, ideas, and subjects so they may be developed later on, with your input. The details and specifics are not part of this exercise. *The Big Bang Project* needs to be a simple, quick read. The first phase is meant to propose a common platform of expression, to begin a process of positive change.

Experts and amateurs from different fields are encouraged to confirm or refute my ideas, or even propose better solutions.

I certainly do not claim to have all the answers, but I do ask better questions, leading to better solutions. You will probably not agree with all my views; that's to be expected. My goal is to initiate a reaction from everyone who wants to get involved in the process of positive change.

Thank you for your curiosity, open mind, and desire for a better world.

*Luc Goulet*

# INTRODUCTION

I often find myself wondering how a truly evolved society would function. We all agree that humans have a lot of work before getting there. There are so many aberrations for a supposedly evolved species: widespread poverty, political and religious wars, deep divisions that are increasingly polarized, human exploitation in all forms, the presence of corruption at just about every level of government, and more. Our planet cries for help by giving us evident warnings. We waste valuable resources (natural and human). The list is too exhaustive to completely enumerate, but we all agree that there is much to be ashamed of. Who can really be proud of mankind's present state of evolution?

Aren't we too smart as individuals to act so stupidly as a collective? We all want to change the world. Each of us wishes for a better path, and we all have ideas for improving something.

# Aren't we too smart as individuals to act so stupidly as a collective?

*The Big Bang Project* offers a positive approach to mankind's future possibilities, triggering our next phase of evolution by creating humanity's best-case scenario.

We often associate evolution with scientific advancements. Science and technology have certainly provided remarkable innovations for society in the past decades. We have clearly demonstrated that mankind is a very intelligent species—and that we can achieve remarkable things.

*The Big Bang Project* is about other spheres of evolution. Many would agree that there are many improvements needed in regard to humanity's evolution in politics, capitalism, and social behaviors. There is an enormous gap between our scientific innovations and social issues. We need to reinvent ourselves to become the truly evolved species we aspire to be. Science has progressed so rapidly because it constantly questions itself based on new ideas and hypotheses that are shared and discussed among the science community and at large.

I believe that rethinking our economic and democratic models has become a general consensus and an emergency. More people are expressing their frustrations throughout all continents. It is time for action to force change.

We can enter a phase where the best of mankind prevails. This is not a utopian concept of an unobtainable ideal world; it is a possible tangent of a future closer to our dreams and true potential.

This is great era. It is ours. We are all responsible for the next generations. Let's be remembered as *the* generation that brought hope.

The technology is at our disposal to make any idea be seen or heard worldwide in an instant. If a pen is mightier than a sword, the web has more impact than any bomb. How can we utilize this incredible communication technology to best serve us? The great strength in numbers can create trends, which can become influential movements that evolve into new ways of thinking.

## THE VISION

I strongly believe that the essence of mankind is good, but there are exceptions. The media gives too much attention to the worst of humanity. The focus of *The Big Bang Project* is on the silent majority of good people; it gives them a common platform to express their ideas. It is a window for all positive actions. How inspiring it can be when you see the best of us under one roof. John Lennon said, "Imagine all the people."

The "big bang" this project hopes to ignite is the great explosion of good and common sense that can happen when all the positive energies unite, multiply, and merge. We can then obtain a critical mass where its core's gravity pulls in more positive energies—to the point that it radiates enough to impact all of us.

## THE MISSION

The Big Bang Project is all about creating a common platform for positive evolution of the three great forces: individuals and society, the Left, and the Right. This book presents ways to rethink the behaviors and responsibilities of these three great entities in a new formula. For real change to happen, these three great spheres of influence, which are closely intertwined, need to work in concert toward a common goal.

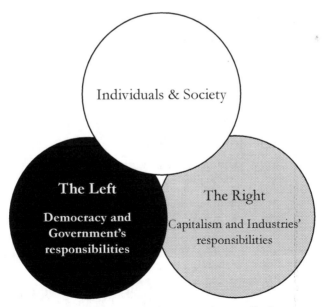

Fig. 1 Interconnection of the great spheres of influence

As the title suggests, the Big Bang Project is not just a book. It is a project with a great mission: triggering the creation of humanity's best-case scenario through a positive approach, where everyone has the opportunity to be part of the conversation and the solution.

The ultimate goal is that every human be free in the true sense: right of expression without political and religious prejudice, right for knowledge and information, right to be an active member of the community by working and earning an honest living (and the possibility of even more), the right of free speech, and the right to believe in any faith (or not).

First, we must form a strong core that will attract many. Each of us represents the essence of the energy the core needs. Let's remember that we all can make a true difference. Our individual actions can have a great impact. The possibility of change is real when there is a common will and a unified effort.

The Big Bang Project suggests that the future of mankind should rest on the people, not on private institutions, religion, or governments.

The ultimate power belongs to us, the individuals forming a society. Politicians constantly make surveys to know our intensions, but they don't ask the questions that can lead society to real changes. They encourage partisanship to the point of increased polarization, which leads to a stalemate and feeds their own political agenda. Governments of all levels are hired by us, paid by us, and work for us. Who's the real boss?

Companies need our clientele; they pay a fortune in advertising to learn more about us. Let's feed them our expectations. We can greatly influence corporations by changing our buying habits. Believe me, they'll react.

**The ultimate power belongs to us, the individuals forming a society.**

Of course, how can we ask the Left and the Right to change if we do not make an effort to change ourselves? We must show that it all starts with the recognition that each of us needs to try to become a better human being. We must open our minds and hearts and wear our "Humble Human" hats (premise proposed later).

*A better me equals a better we,*
*A better we equals a better me.*

The path that *The Big Bang Project* proposes is one that allows continual improvement. There is no one magic solution to all our mishaps, but many steps in the right direction can equal giant leaps.

# CHAPTER 1

# HUMAN EVOLUTION: CAN WE DO BETTER?

To say that today's reality is different from the time when all our systems in place were created is an understatement. No one from these different eras in Europe and America could have imagined our challenges in this day and age.

How could our Founding Fathers have foreseen the extremely complex reality of the twenty-first century? Transport, trade, communications, and media have made the world more accessible and more interconnected than ever imagined. Multiculturalism has spread worldwide; diversities in cultures and religions cohabit and blend in the same communities. Problems pertain to the great growth of population: pollution to the extent of creating important environmental issues, such as climate change. Natural resources are not so abundant anymore. Countries on the verge of bankruptcy have significant repercussions across continents. Extremists and terrorism change the face and parameters of war.

Our ancestors thought of and invented laws, democracy, capitalism, and economic policies. Even spiritual and religious convictions and beliefs date back many more centuries. These ways may have served their purpose in their time, but they are all clearly outdated in today's world.

Some would argue that there have been changes over the years. But is it true progress when the deciders make these changes to gradually give them an increasing advantage? Who has been better served thanks to the changes: the decision makers or society in general?

These factors explain why it is expected that we have gone astray from the original intent of the different models, and we need to realign our ways with the challenges of the moment and tomorrow.

The proof is in the results. The unemployment rates across the world are at critical levels, and the economies of many countries are precarious. There are political stalemates in most democratic countries, and wealth distribution is seriously questioned. Dissatisfaction and disillusion are common themes. Most have a pessimistic view of humanity's future.

Pointing fingers and trying to find guilty parties is not part of the discussion here. Peaceful change cannot happen through revolutions that result in harmful confrontations. Expressing our discontent is one thing; we need to get to the next level. Trying to find a better way is the real challenge. Let's discuss in terms of solutions, not complaints. Problems are really symptoms. Finding the root cause and repairing the core reason is the greater goal.

The systems in place will be questioned; new ideas will be proposed to begin a constructive conversation toward positive change that is decided by the people for the people. I do not proclaim to possess all the answers. I simply want to offer the best strategy for positive evolution.

**Let's discuss in terms of solutions, not complaints.**

All governing concepts are long due for a "reset" from bottom up. In management terms, the systems in place need a *Kaizen* (a Japanese business model first created for improving efficiency and productivity where everybody is periodically consulted). The accent is put on listening to the workers of all levels for ideas and feedback. The theory is that people on different levels understand their realities and needs better than anyone in the upper scales of responsibility. No organization can advance toward a common goal when departments work in a silo; everything and everyone are interrelated. We can learn much from all members of the hierarchy. In our case, everybody can and should get involved.

First, we need a plan. We need to be open-minded, to ask "What if?" with no partisanship. *It starts by finding the better questions to find the better answers.*

The age-old question about the Right or Left is wrong. Every society functions with both in different forms. The real question should be: how can the Left *and* Right best serve society as partners, not rivals?

# CHAPTER 2
# PREMISES FOR A POSITIVE EVOLUTION

Fig. 2 Premises for positive evolution

Humanity's capacity to transmit information and knowledge to the next generations is how we have evolved. But some questionable points of view are also transmitted from generation to generation, and we are tempted to accept them as truth. We hate because our parents and their parents hated; we divide because our elders divided. We fight because that's what we've been taught. We have learned from our forbearers to disapprove of anything that's different. They judged what they didn't understand; should we do the same?

To achieve the next level of mankind's evolution, we must reprogram our wrongly based interpretations. We need to turn these negative and destructive behaviors into positive experiences. Just like a child victim of violence who is likely to repeat the same violent behavior until he or she finally breaks the pattern, we need to move forward as a society. We need to stop this unjustified never-ending cycle of violence; it has brought us nowhere we want to be.

What's the most important enemy of evolution? How we handle diversity is our biggest obstacle and our most important failure. From hatred, we are trying to evolve to acceptance and tolerance. We more or less disapprove, but we'll live with it. We should instead fast-forward our evolution to *appreciation* and *embracing the difference*.

Diversity is expressed in many forms: religious, cultural, political, ethnic, economic, and sexual orientation, just to name a few. Too often, these differences have been the source of tension, mistrust, prejudice, ignorance, and judgment. Diversity has continued to be an important pretext for many deep divisions, even wars, for so many years.

As a premise for success, we must leave all these negative vibes toward what is different behind: prejudice, skepticism, blind partisanship, fear, ignorance, preconceived notions of superiority or inferiority, and any form of violence, intolerance, or exclusion. You can shift from a negative approach to positive by wearing the "Humble Human" hat. The interpretation wheel will then turn to curiosity, wanting more information and knowledge, and understanding the benefits from new perspectives.

**How we handle diversity is our biggest obstacle and our most important failure.**

They say that only fools don't change their minds, so don't be a fool. Accept that you must change, I must change, and we all must change our perspective on diversity. Our biases are based on ignorance and fed with unjustified hatred passed on.

We all wear different hats (real or virtual), according to circumstances. For example, I will sometimes choose my "Cirque du Soleil" hat. When I need to unload the car and it should be done in two trips, I'll take the challenge and try to do it in one. I then become a pretend artist of Cirque du Soleil. The one trip turns into a great balancing act where every move is calculated to perfection. With the mind-set that comes with my virtual hat, my predisposition and concentration levels are at their peak. Without, I would have probably broken my neck more than once.

## THE HUMBLE HUMAN PERSPECTIVE

This time, take a moment to try my Humble Human hat—one size fits all.

It comes with these thoughts:

*I am humble before the universe, for its immensity beyond my comprehension. It holds so many mysteries we may never unlock.*

*I am humble before our galaxy, for it hides countless diverse wonders we have yet to explore and understand.*

*I am humble before Earth, for its incredible diversity, the awesome delicate balance of nature, its great power, and all it provides.*

*I am humble before mankind, for its great resilience, ingenuity, creativity, and diversity.*

*I am humble before you, for all the skills, talent, knowledge, and experiences you possess that I don't.*

*I am humble before my own potential, the life I have, all that I can do and give, and how my ideas, inspirations, and actions can make a great difference.*

*I am humble before the opportunity of learning from you, sharing, and contributing with you to make this world a better place.*

With these thoughts in mind, it becomes easier to appreciate diversity. It is what makes the universe, nature, and our individuality. We all complement each other; this is our biggest strength. Thank you for being different and unique; you add new colors and nuances that we can all benefit from. I can only grow from the inspirations given by your distinctive perspective. I need to recognize and embrace the fact that, even though I possess unique skills and ideas, there are many people—from every race, society, gender, and faith—who are smarter, stronger, and more talented than me. And we are all better for it.

Stay away from extremes. We must not wave any religious or political flags with extreme partisanship.

Extreme ideologies make evolution practically impossible. The blind partisanship will never accept arguments from the opposed camp; they're always right, and the rest are always wrong. Extremists of all sides all have this in common: ignorance, lack of empathy, and closed minds. They prefer to divide, and they have no motivation to compromise. This is comparable to the attitude of someone who has been brainwashed. These people are part of the problem, and they are definitely not welcomed in the solution process.

Only positive interventions are allowed. The Big Bang Project wants to demonstrate that good brings good. Just as a smile attracts a smile, positive actions come back as positive experiences for both the giver and the receiver.

We are all cohabitants of the same beautiful and fragile planet. Let's all make the best of it together as partners, not as adversaries. "We are the world. We are the children." I can't resist quoting superb songs because they have the capacity to touch us deeply and bring us all closer. Their popularity is a proof among many that humans are good.

I strongly believe there is a majority of sensible people of all political and religious agendas who are willing to unite for a greater cause. We can all put aside—or at least restrain—our partisanship.

In the next chapter, I will demonstrate that a lot of great people are doing great things, and a lot of "ordinary" people are doing extraordinary things. The problem is that we don't hear enough about them. We can recognize a killer because all the media coverage made him or her famous, but we don't know who our local and international heroes are.

We will be inspired by them, and we will recognize that giving *what* you can, *how* you can, and *when* you can makes you a better person. *You* will benefit from your good actions.

# CHAPTER 3

# A BETTER ME, A BETTER WE—AND VICE VERSA

## WHAT COMES AFTER THE "ME, MYSELF, AND I" ERA?

For a few decades, personal growth has been a very popular topic. Many great books have been written, and great motivational speakers have mobilized many people into becoming better people with better lives. All that is great; I'm a big fan of Anthony Robbins. He has motivated thousands, including famous and important people. I love how *The Secret* explains all the potential we have, how to tap into our inner strength, and more. I strongly believe that striving to become a better human being is an ongoing necessary quest in order to evolve. There must be an evolutionary phase after the "me, myself, and I" era.

The better we each are, the more equipped we become to provide for ourselves and our families—and to help the community. In return, helping others will contribute greatly into becoming better human beings. The rewards of giving are countless.

Another undeniable fact that proves that mankind is good is the contrast between someone who has witnessed and lived a horror like war and someone coming back from a humanitarian mission. The person who has endured death and destruction created by armies comes back with a broken soul. Post-traumatic stress syndrome is often the result, and reentering society is a challenge for many. A person seeing great destruction made by nature, volunteering and providing care to others, comes back from this experience replenished with a positive energy and a sense of fulfillment and pride. He or she has seen despair, but the main focus was hope and help.

The Beatles sang, "We all want to change the world." But we all feel powerless. We think the task is too great, and we don't quite know where to begin or what to do. The most important objective of the Big Bang Project is giving people the opportunity to change their lives for the better by finding the right cause and the right way to connect.

Real differences can be made rapidly. People can organize, rally, and react much faster than governments or big private institutions. To change things, we must first rely on ourselves, and the powerful establishments will follow.

There is much we can do without the intervention of the government. Already large and worldwide goodwill organizations and foundations exist. Already we have proven through natural catastrophes how we can mobilize ourselves to help people in need.

## THE GREAT POWER OF GIVING

Many successful people have used their power and influence to take matters in their own hands, and they are now great philanthropists. More proof of the good of humanity.

**People can organize, rally, and react much faster than governments or big private institutions.**

Many examples of people reaching the greater levels of success in their careers have progressed to become even better human beings. More influential personalities take charge and contribute by doing it themselves through great organizations they created to directly help people who need our attention. I call these great individuals "superheroes."

More and more people who have achieved greatness are giving back more than ever, yet some blame them for their success. While some critics argue that they should pay a higher percentage of taxes, I ask how much in "absolute dollar amount" they have contributed. The percentage may be smaller than some would expect, but it still translates to enormous dollar amounts. I need to ask how much sales tax they have paid in one year. I must take into account all the jobs they created and the input their business activities generated in the economy. On top of that, they are significant philanthropists. Can you say the same? How does your total "absolute dollar amount" contribution compare? How much of your time is given for the community compared to these busy individuals? If they can find the time, shouldn't we?

Wealth is not a commodity for anyone to take. Wealth is created and earned by people who have a vision, a mission, and the leadership to make their dreams a reality. By doing so, they create employment, new business opportunities are born, and the economy grows. Bravo.

I would like to thank, in the name of all of us, the incredible individuals who have contributed more in one year than most could achieve in a lifetime: Bill Gates, Warren Buffet, Sir Richard Branson, Ted Turner, Oprah, Bono, Sean Penn, Angelina Jolie, Brad Pitt, Celine Dion and René, Sirs Paul McCartney and Sting, John Bon Jovi, Al Gore, Bill Clinton, Andre Agassi, and Magic Johnson. The list goes on and on. Exemplary citizens are taking initiatives to better our world. They deserve to be honored for their social contributions and inspiration. They didn't have to, but they did.

The money and effort they put toward their causes help people directly. I wonder if the impact on society would be as important if they had put all that money into extra taxes for the government.

A lot of not-so-famous people are doing astonishing things. Ordinary folks are achieving the extraordinary out there. We seldom get a chance to see these incredible people. Thanks to "CNN Heroes," a beautiful gala held every year, we get to see real-life heroes. People like you and me are making our world a better place. I'm extremely humbled and moved by the greatness of these individuals who have found important causes and done something about them. They have become superheroes by helping so many and inspiring others for action.

A *spark* is what I call any good deed, good idea, kind gesture, or helping hand. These *sparks* are shining a light of hope for mankind. When they are scattered, they do not have the same strength as when they are grouped. When we hear of a *spark*, we are encouraged and inspired, but the light fades when we stop hearing about it.

Become a hero yourself. Join the cause that speaks to you. The list of rewards will surprise you. Here are just a random few:

- gratifying feelings of accomplishment
- making new friends who share the same passion
- best solution to avoid boredom and loneliness
- learning new skills and discovering hidden talents
- pride when you see how you have impacted the lives of real people
- recognition by all that you are part of the solution
- the legacy you leave behind, the values you teach, and the inspiration you bring to your children, friends, and neighbors
- the things you learn, the places you go, and the people you meet
- contacts who may help your career
- future contributions of those you helped
- knowing you have become a better human being

**Become a hero yourself. Join the cause that speaks to you.**

- lessons you learn, seeing how so many people live in difficult conditions and still find ways to smile, making room for kindness, and putting your reality into perspective
- it can even help against depression and prevent suicide by giving the chance to restart people's lives, ignite a *spark*, and find a new, positive purpose
- you may find your soul mate

Need I say more? The advantages of giving can be priceless. Listen to the real volunteers' testimonials on the Big Bang Project's website. They will surely inspire you. They all have this in common: *the rewards outweigh the efforts.*

Shouldn't it be part of our teens' education? The call to action for good should be learned at a young age. Think how our world would be different if all children at every school learned how to participate. Think of the valuable lessons children of both camps would learn. It can be fun to give. Kids need to have a good time—even those living in poverty. What if our children donated musical instruments, Frisbees, books, and Rubik's Cubes? The kids could play together and develop new skills. Think of the bond the children would develop. A new generation of children who understand the reality of less fortunate people won't judge; they will help others.

Retired people may find a new purpose and enjoy the friendship while being part of the solution. Boredom is often felt when people retire. Retired people can still contribute while having fun. They can live their passions in many ways that can make a difference.

An employer has the choice between two equivalent candidates: one has done some volunteering and has praise from the organization, and the other has not. Who is likely to get picked? Communication and organizational skills acquired in a volunteering experience are useful in the workplace.

Those who receive social welfare should be encouraged to give back to the community by contributing at least a few hours per week. New opportunities may come out of it. Getting active is the best way to keep your body and mind in the best condition and to be ready and able to reenter the job market. Pride as a contributing factor in your region is not exclusive to the employed.

If we divide all the national, state or provincial, and municipal social expenses equally per habitant of a country, the average cost per person is often superior to one's contribution. Everyone may become a positive social contributor even though his or her share of taxes is below the actual cost, simply by being part of a charitable organization.

Serving one's country must be about more than joining the army. There are so many possibilities for leaving your mark. You don't need to make it mandatory when all the advantages and rewards speak for themselves.

## ONE PLATFORM—ALL THE OPTIONS

What if we show all the good causes, foundations, and volunteering organizations in one place? Big or small, local or international, we could learn about them and see what they have accomplished, their next objectives, and what we could do to help. All people would find causes that touched them and ways to help that are just right for them. The scattered *sparks* become one huge, shining, continuous light that radiates enough for everyone to see.

Every organization of goodwill may apply to be presented on the Big Bang Project's website. Your organization will be displayed in this superb platform where as many foundations as possible can be heard of and helped.

Many big corporations give enormous amounts through foundations they created or are associated with. The Big Bang Project could be an excellent window for extra visibility.

There are many methods to contribute; giving money is not the only way. Your time, talents, skills, ideas, and inspirations are just as important—if not more.

Imagine if each of us found the perfect organization and the perfect type of contribution. Imagine how many people would commit to volunteering one six-hour day per month—twelve days per year. Multiply that by the number of participants, and you have thousands of extra productive days for your community and the world.

**What if we show all the good causes, foundations, and volunteering organizations in one place?**

In a community of 200,000 people, if 10 percent of the population decides to join and give twelve days of volunteering per year, it amounts to 240,000 days of contributions. Think of what can be done in 240,000 days for a community of 200,000 souls. Wow!

Imagine how greater numbers could be reached with the addition of an additional 1 percent of the population. Add one more day of volunteering per year, and it adds up. Every day given to volunteering makes a difference in your community.

It's like working out or choosing a sport you like to get in shape. Once you've got a routine settled, you can't stop. The better you get, the more you love it—and the more you want to do it. The more good results you get, the more encouraged you become to pursue.

The Big Bang Project is *the* website for presenting all the possibilities for doing real good. The organizations can explain what they do, where, for whom, what they need, and how you can help. You are sure to find something you connect with.

The Big Bang Project also offers a platform for expression. If you are an artist, you are encouraged to choose what moves you to inspire us with your art. A song, painting, picture, poem, or sculpture can move, have the great power to inspire, and unite many.

I believe in mankind because of how people with great messages of hope have made such an impact. Gandhi, Nelson Mandela, Martin Luther King, and the Dalai Lama have moved the entire planet. Again, the importance and timeless attention we give to these people in our history is for their message of a better world and peace that we all wish for. That says a lot about us.

The Big Bang Project unites all those who believe in the messages of peace given by these great visionaries. Their sacrifices were not in vain; thanks to today's communication technology, we can unify our actions to finally realize the dreams of a better world to share. Be remembered for your accomplishments and social contributions. Take part in the movement the Big Bang Project proposes.

Our social responsibilities do not end here. Democracy and capitalism must also evolve. We each play a key role in the changes needed to evolve. In the next chapters, we will discuss the necessary improvements required in the systems in place and our individual accountabilities.

We will determine the best behaviors for creating a positive impact. We all have opinions about how to improve. Your comments and ideas will be encouraged. Your opinion counts, and it is crucial for influencing change. Take part in the conversation, help us find better questions, and lead us closer to the right answers.

## IDEA FOR A SUPER REALITY TV SHOW

The popularity of reality TV could be made to good use. What if every country had a TV reality show where six to ten candidates would each represent a goodwill organization. There would be three categories: local, national, and international.

Instead of eliminating candidates, those who attract the most people and make the biggest difference would get the bigger monthly prize. The same candidates stay during the whole season. We can witness their progress toward winning the next round. *The idea is to multiply the efforts of good—not to eliminate.* At the end of the season, there are no losers; first, second, and third prizes are distributed.

Specialists, scientists, and philanthropists could participate. They would comment and provide great input on the efforts and results of every participant. The population would vote for their favorite causes. But more importantly, they would be invited to join and get involved with one of the candidates' projects. Talk about participative TV? The audience may participate in the show, and they would be encouraged to do so.

Even candidates who were not picked for the show could be seen on the show's website. During the season, one of these first unselected candidates could join the show.

Artists could join the party and offer talent and inspiration. They have the power and influence to transform this show into a great event. By creating a buzz around the idea of helping and giving, we all win. I welcome TV producers to act. I won't be greedy about royalties.

## EDUCATION VERSUS KNOWLEDGE

The possibilities of learning and getting information have been completely transformed since the Internet came along. This opportunity must come with the great mission of making learning accessible to all.

Traditional education is a privilege too many children (and adults) do not have. The cost of traditional scholarship is very important. The price of building schools, maintenance, administration, and having enough qualified teachers with enough time for every student is too high for too many. *It is more possible, and less expensive, to bring knowledge to each than to bring everyone to schools.*

We now have the possibility to offer all students a choice of teachers for every subject. Students may choose more than one teacher per topic. Whereas schools can only offer one teacher for twenty or more students. If a student does not connect with that teacher's methods or personality, it's just too bad!

Education should not be a gift reserved to a fortunate few; it should be considered an essential like food, water, clothing, and shelter. The greatest evolutionary step for mankind is getting rid of ignorance on a planetary scale. Unfortunately, it can't happen with traditional education; knowledge must spread in new ways.

Traditional educational has suffered a high rate of male dropouts. What if the web offered an alternative for knowledge sharing—through the child's passions—with many different teachers and ways to learn? The best method for catching someone's interest in learning is encouraging passion. It leads to curiosity and the continual search for more knowledge. Can't we make learning fun?

What if developed countries' children with the opportunity to attend school made videos of their classes and make them available on the Internet? What if we sent our old computers, smartphones, and tablets to those who cannot afford a communication device? A few children could share one device. Let's bring knowledge, information, and a new form of education to all since all can't get to it. The recycling of used technology is a challenge for rich

**It is more possible, and less expensive, to bring knowledge to each than to bring everyone to schools.**

countries that crave the newest technology. Too many communication devices are useless when they could be serving.

We need to invent new ways to spread information and recognize acquired skills via different forms of educational tools. Self-sufficiency starts with knowledge.

Why can't we create specialized certification or diplomas for people who study specific subjects by other means than traditional education? If they pass the required exams without going to school, isn't that equivalent?

Offering an opportunity to learn is the best way to provide hope, and it is a positive alternative to crime and violence.

There is so much that can be achieved if we all realize that we each play an essential role in society. The next chapter will present new ideas, including a possible path to improve how democracy is expressed and how governments can evolve to better serve society. Again, we will look at how individuals and society can impact governmental decisions.

# CHAPTER 4

# SHOULD GOVERNMENTS AND DEMOCRACY EVOLVE?

Democracy is by far the best social system there is. The vision for governing is noble: power to the people.

It is the only model where the population decides who will represent them and manage common services and expenses. People vote according to the vision and promises of politicians. In theory, once elected, the government works for all its citizens to best execute what was promised. In theory, things are supposed to get done.

In reality, the beautiful model is somewhat altered. The science of political tactics takes over, and its first victim is democracy. The model is replaced by divided parties whose ultimate objective is political gain. The population is pushed aside by lobbyists, political strategies, constant power struggles, and promises made to special contributors. As a result, few projects are realized, and politicians take on endless arguments to distract us from concrete issues. Blind partisanship has led governments to political stalemates more often than achieving their real goals.

Fig. 3 Right or Left?

The country that represents the model of democracy throughout the world has turned it into a spectacle. It has evolved into a war of negative advertising between two clans. A politician's job is to get the most money through fundraising activities, not contradict the party line, and discredit everything from the opposing party. Personal issues get more attention than solving real problems. It seems they are spending less time doing actual work for the population than on their own careers.

Both parties sit on old ideological arguments that will never be settled, like an endless loop, all in their favor, purposely dividing the population. Health care was an election issue that led the losing party to disrespect the founding principle of democracy by constantly trying to block the wish of the majority to have a public health-care system. Their ultimate political goal is that the program fails. Instead, they should be working *with* the leading party to make it the best possible public health-care system.

What led to the fiscal cliff was like an old television soap where each politician was playing a predictable role. When there's a cliff ahead, you don't want the leaders to constantly argue about whether they should turn left or right until it's too late and the damage is done.

Most, if not all, democratic countries are in the same predicament— if not worse. Mismanagement has led many nations to the verge of bankruptcy and an exaggerated national debt. Corruption is also far too present. Is it surprising that people have become discouraged? The credibility of most politicians should be seriously questioned. Mistrusting politicians is the common sentiment.

Even those who enter politics with the best intentions for the people and noble dreams to serve are faced with a system that forces them to "play the game." That counterproductive political environment is enough to make any leader's hair turn gray in no time.

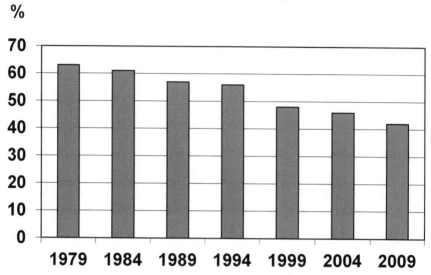

Fig. 4 Election turnout in Europe

Election turnouts have declined over the years in much of Europe. The United States has also shown relatively low turnouts compared to the top-performing countries. On November 10, 2014, Jose A. Del Real of *The Washington Post* wrote, "Voter turnout in 2014 was the lowest since WW II."

People who choose not to vote, cancel their votes, or simply vote for the wrong reasons are too common. It has also become a question of image and advertising budget, very little substance. The party with the biggest advertising budget is likely to win the election. A large percentage of TV ads are now using the strategy of "negative advertising," focusing on bashing the competition.

Is the present political system the ultimate way to express democracy? Does it still serve its intended purpose? We have to think not.

This situation has been going on for too long, and it seems to be getting worse. There must be important changes in the political system to ensure that true democracy is expressed, instead of the political dead end we are at.

It is our responsibility, as employers of people working for all levels of government, to decide what is expected of them in the mandate we pay them for.

With our present communication technology, can there be more involvement of the population than voting every four years? It was impossible for the Founding Fathers to imagine that feedback could be done on a massive scale (and on a regular basis). The system created back then was the best they could do with the technology they had. Now things have changed; we can include the population in the decision-making process more than ever.

Today's world is in a continuous change and evolution. Domestic or international, the issues are more numerous and complex than ever. Let's think about how we can create a better system that could adapt and be proactive to the constantly evolving challenges.

The model can be improved to come closer to the true commitment of democracy, allowing the population to get more involved in the decision-making process.

The Big Bang Project is about reaching mankind's next phase of evolution. Democracy is an important aspect of our future. All our nation's shared goals and services deserve the best governing methods available. We are presently losing too much productivity and efficiency. Our hard-earned money cannot go to waste like that; we can't afford it.

The following issues are intended to serve as a starting point to reinventing democracy. Topics proposed are never part of the questions on the multiple surveys political parties give, but they need to be addressed. The Big Bang Project's first phase has an objective of finding the right questions to ask to finally obtain the best solutions. Your feedback in great numbers can make it happen. The next issues should be considered as a trigger to begin a new conversation.

Remove any partisanship hat you might be wearing, and put on the open-minded hat. If we could start from scratch and invent a new set of ways of doing politics, what would it look like?

## MANAGEMENT

Can you imagine any important corporation being run the way our governments are? Our elected decision makers have opposing political agendas; their first wish is that the other fails. They are unlikely to reach a constructive consensus. Does it look like an efficient and productive management team working together toward a common vision, mission, and objective?

Some say you can't run a country like a company. The context is quite different; the goals are not similar. But top management principles are transferable from any entity that is seeking maximum efficiency in all departments. The main task of any management team is to plan, organize, give directives, and control. They must minimize expenses but get optimal results, constantly revising their strategies to improve.

The management team must ensure that all departments and employees of all levels share the same vision. Seeking constant improvements, it always pursues new ideas and methods. To ensure maximum efficiency, management must find the best possible candidates; each must be specifically qualified and suited

**Can you imagine any important corporation being run the way our governments are?**

for the task. Elected officials must connect the dots, making sure that no department works in silo, understanding they are all connected by the global vision decided by the voters. They have to mobilize all its people to best serve its population. Diversity of opinions is encouraged so that no angles are left unexplored. People with different views will complement each other and find the perfect compromise. Growth is the ongoing mission of any administration.

## COMPETENCE

Would credible management in any important organization choose to transfer the director of marketing to human resources and the finance director to marketing? What leader, in any management context, would decide to have someone running a department without specialized higher experience and knowledge about that specific department? Unfortunately, this is the case in my country—and probably in yours to.

Each ministry should be composed of expertise that complements each other for the best possible decisions, taking into account all pertinent points of view. The candidates must have credible experience in the appointed field; politics should be a complementary skill.

The head minister of every department, with the assistance of the chief executive, should appoint a dream team to manage it. The population should then approve this dream team. For example, an industry leader, a management generalist (e.g., MBA), an environmentalist from the science community, a finance and/or legal expert, an economist, an international trade expert, and a specialist in human resources, and/or a sociologist (when social issues are at stake) can form a group of decision makers working toward the objectives fixed by the department head minister and the president. Each department would need a tailor-made team for its particular needs. We should analyze every ministry to determine what would constitute the perfect dream team for each.

## TRANSPARENCY, ACCOUNTABILITY, AND A STRICT CODE OF ETHICS

Any credible management recognizes the importance of accountability toward coworkers, suppliers, and ultimately the shareholders and customers. Any business leader understands that the customer is the most important reason the business exists. Customer satisfaction is a measure that all organizations take very seriously. The difference is that in democracy, the population is both shareholder and customer of the governments (sometimes also a supplier). It is normal to ask for total accountability from all public officials and their employees. Politicians' transparency means that we need the proper tools to measure their performances. We, as a society, must decide what information our governments give.

Corruption exists because the system in place allows politicians to become corrupt. Let's ask ourselves how we can change the system so there is no room for greed.

## RESPONSIBILITIES

We elect and pay public officials to ensure that all systems in place work at maximum efficiency, to the satisfaction of those who receive any services. Do you feel that it's being achieved in your country?

Secondly, we demand that electoral issues, ongoing priorities, and objectives for improvements are executed promptly. Can we say this is happening today?

We need the government to create the perfect environment to encourage growth for the private sector. It is responsible for making sure that the industries respect their social responsibilities, such as respect for the environment.

There must never be hidden agendas or special favors. All details of public expenses are to be public knowledge. Efficiency reports must be revealed periodically. Only issues are subjects of conversations; negative personal attacks are not tolerated.

Politicians spend time doing what we pay them for. Any other activities, such as fundraising, political PR, and electoral speeches, must be executed outside the normal week's work schedule.

We also ask that they represent our country internationally in a way that would make us proud to be its citizens.

## POLITICAL PARTIES AND INDEPENDENTS

In the old days, the complexity of issues was simpler. Choices for the population were made simple: vote for your favorite party or candidate. Different political parties could represent all the alternatives. The technology would not permit elections or referendums at will. Democracy was expressed in a simple matter. We get to vote every four years or so by marking an X on a ballet. Compiling more data would have been impossible to do back then. Choosing a party was the simplest method for making democracy a reality. Is it still the best way? Is democracy compromised by simplifying the decision-making process to satisfy limits from the past?

**Does it make sense to divide all the different issues and challenges into two (or rarely more than three) parties?**

Today, the system of political parties keeps us away from advancing on a clear, well-defined path for every separate issue. Does it make sense to divide all the different issues and challenges into two (or rarely more than three) parties? Can social, economic, defense, education, health, and cultural issues be bundled into one set of views for every party? Doesn't it narrow the options? Aren't there more possibilities in one issue than there are political parties? With all the different subjects and opportunities for each, is it even mathematically possible that anyone, politician or voter, can adhere to one party line that is right on everything? Does it make sense that moderate views are in the same group as extreme positions?

Political parties have divided into clans that are meant to create counterproductive partisanships. Different interpretations and perspectives often divide the clans. This creates scenarios where a politician's speech

31

will be different in the beginning of the electoral process to please the party's core influence. The speech changes to attract a different set of voters. Is this honesty or political tactics?

That division among the political parties results in frequent dead ends when it's time to settle an issue. It is practically impossible to progress at the best possible pace in this environment. Is it normal that the entire dynamic is transformed when a party has the majority? When a party gets the majority, it can disregard any ideas from opposing parties. If the party is elected with a minority, the other party seems to block everything. Not many advances are made. Different scenarios of execution for different situations is an excuse we accept, but it leaves too much room for political tactics instead of complete efficiency—no matter the political landscape—after elections.

The issues must matter more than a team. Partisanship for a team is great in sports, but it has no place in government's decision-making procedures. It cannot be about competition between rival teams; it should be about teamwork for finding the best solutions.

Don't we need and want our politicians to be totally free of expression on every subject? Wouldn't it make more sense that they'd be truly honest about their own perspectives versus a party's view? If someone has a great idea but does not belong to an important political party, will he be heard?

If our politicians were independents, the discussions would exclusively be on each separate issue. All the precious time, effort, and money wasted on political strategies would be eliminated and replaced by constructive conversations for concrete results.

Some independents could represent themselves for the presidency—with sets of skills and experiences that are suited for the job. Others could represent themselves for a specific department. They would have specialized know-how, experience, and understanding of the issues and challenges of that department. This way, we would have the right person at the right place—and the right place for the right person. At last.

## NEUTRALITY

The dream team running the country needs to get things done, and they must show more neutrality. The context of political parties encourages just the opposite.

Elected officials must leave their old political parties behind and become part of the executive team. If our leaders were free from the imposed mind-set of a political party, they would become more negotiable in the issues. The deep divisions between parties make it almost impossible to work with diverging arguments.

Politicians have proven that they are not ready to trade their old partisanship hats for the "open-minded-for-compromise" hat and come to a consensus that makes sense for all. It would be considered going against the system.

## PARTY FUNDING AND ADVERTISING

The concept of *added value* must be applied for all government spending. Added value means that for the extra money spent, there must be, as close as possible, the equivalent value received. Who should benefit from this added value—the politicians' personal career goals or the taxpayers and communities?

The enormous sums being spent on political advertising budgets are very questionable. No added value is given to the population. Most of these donations to political parties have a specific purpose: getting something in return. Again, we pay indirectly for many special favors given to important donors to the political parties, and we receive nothing.

Is it fair when advertising budgets outweigh substance? Do we really want people's votes to be influenced by negative attacks and repetitive advertisements instead of convincing arguments?

I see only three possible options to rectify the problem:

- *Replace political parties with independents.*
  As you probably have guessed, this is my preferred option. On top of all the reasons mentioned above, there would be no need for special party funding. We could at last have constructive conversations only about issues. Each candidate would have the equivalent media coverage, website, and social media. This would ensure that their arguments are heard.

- *Abolish or limit all party funding and advertising.*
  If we abolish party funding and give equal TV coverage to all parties and/or independents, substance becomes a must. Irrelevant attacks would not be permitted. The game would at least be fair for all participants. The size of the wallet would not give any advantage to anyone. Isn't that better democracy? We want real information—not pointless advertising that is seldom really informative and rarely specific about issues.

  Politicians give too much time and effort to fundraising. This is very unproductive for a society. The game of giving back to special party contributors has a probable cost much to important for the population to keep paying.

- *Use all that money and reinvest it directly into a cause the political party stands for.*
  At least the money would go back to the population. A better way for politicians to gain popularity is to work on fundraising efforts for concrete causes and humanitarian organizations. They would benefit from the extra coverage for good actions. The added value would be shared with the communities.

Sponsoring companies would gain positive advertising and a better public image—a win-win-win situation.

## THE VOTING SYSTEM

We have had the same voting method for a very long time. We need to upgrade our voting system to better reflect today's reality and possibilities.

## ELECTORAL PROCESS

The electoral process seems to take longer than it should. Candidates spend a fortune on advertising. They travel across the country to give the same speeches. The speeches are void of specifics and are inefficient. The entire procedure requires too much unproductive work—instead of honoring their true mandate. It is far too expensive for what we get in return.

The reality of yesteryear demanded such time and travel. Today, with traditional media coverage added to social media and websites, the messages could be heard by the entire population in less than a fraction of the time and travel it presently takes.

Once elected, politicians are welcome to travel to resolve real regional issues—but not for political gain. A lot of useless time and wasted money is coming from our pockets. Every dollar must be treated with the utmost respect for its contributors. Do you sense that this is presently the case?

## UP-TO-DATE TECHNOLOGY

Isn't it surprising that the way we vote has practically not changed in decades? Do we really need to ask people to go to a voting booth and wait in line for a while? Is it a productive day when companies have to deal with the logistics of giving time off to all employees to vote? Many people don't have the time or motivation to go through the trouble to vote.

As demonstrated earlier, voting turnouts are insufficient in most countries. That's important in any democratic system. We must find a way to increase the percentage of voters so that democracy is expressed by the maximum of the population.

Updated technology is used more and more by the private sector to facilitate transactions. Today's safe environment allows even bank transactions to be made online. An impressive majority of people have their own—or have access to—computers, tablets, game consoles, smartphones, televisions, and watches.

We need to ask the major players in communication technologies like Microsoft, Apple, Google, and Facebook to join forces and create a voting app. They can create a safe app, using a combination of safety features (fingerprints, eye recognition, and special predetermined private questions only the voter can answer). For additional security, a confirmation of vote could be sent to the voter via e-mail or snail mail. This avoids any possible fraud.

If voting were made easy, many more people would use their democratic privilege. Every vote is important. This app would also prevent voided votes because the $X$ mark did not conform to regulations.

## VOTING FOR THE RIGHT REASONS

If we push this idea further, the voting app can provide some kind of information from each candidate (not personal attacks). There is always more than one important issue at stake when considering who to vote for. The voting app could help sort it out by providing a table where issues are listed. It could even have a short plan for each candidate. Voters could decide what importance to put on each issue, and they could identify their favorite candidates by ranking every issue. Once it is completed, the voting app calculates the winner based upon the value given for each question.

## VOTING FOR IMPORTANT ISSUES

If we push this concept even further, one can imagine greater involvement by the population in the decision-making process. What if the population also voted on predetermined issues? A referendum option could provide quick feedback from the people. Instead of making surveys that are sometimes misleading, a proper vote for certain important issues could settle the stalemates we often witness. The voting app could make it possible.

## A PROPER MAJORITY

Many countries are divided by two visions, which represent two opposite parties, and the split among voters is often close to fifty-fifty. This brings a difficult premise for further decisions. One-half of management wants to go left, and the other half wants to turn right, but we never choose one common direction according to each specific issue, based on the excuse of a larger vision.

When you consider the possible margin of error, is 50 percent plus one really a true majority? There are many reasons to suspect that more than a notable percentage of votes come from either blind partisans for one specific party or social cause. They never change without weighing all the issues in the balance. There are also misinformed and undecided people who can be easily influenced by irrelevant negative advertising. Others have their votes voided, don't show up on Election Day, or choose to send a message by voting against the leading party.

**When you consider the possible margin of error, is 50 percent plus one really a true majority?**

The margin should be enough to make sure a true and deserved consensus occurs. The majority should be established between 52 and 55 percent. It could be around 52 percent when voting for political leaders and slightly more for issues. When we analyze surveys, we notice that more often than not, the majority is more convincing on issues than on leaders. Let's work with that. Things need to get done.

Which of the following majority is more convincing?

Fig. 5 50 percent plus one majority

Fig. 6 52 percent to 55 percent majority

What if, for certain major issues, such as amendments, legalization of the consumption of marijuana, gay marriage, going to war or not, the power of vote be given to three entities: president (or prime minister), ministers, and population.

Let's say we give a percentage to each, and the percentage of the population is counted in the balance by acknowledging all votes. For example, we would decide that a total of 60 percent is given to the population, 25 percent to the president, and 15 percent to the ministers. If the vote from the population is split half and half, 30 percent of the total final percentage is given on both sides, then the ministers vote in the same fashion, a split percentage of their 15 percent. Finally the president's vote represents the last 25 percent by him- or herself. If the population agrees at 90 percent, the ministers or the president cannot reverse the decision. Since 90 percent of 60 percent equals 54 percent, this represents a majority.

This method offers a fair balance of power between the population and elected officials. The percentages mentioned above are just examples. We need to choose as a society what the best split of voting percentage is. We could decide to give the population 65 percent, meaning that a majority of 80 percent of the population would suffice to give the final decision to the population.

The idea is to question if democracy could be expressed better, thanks to the new possibilities that technology can offer. This system would enable us to move forward even if there is a stalemate among the population and/or politicians. It also prevents a president and/or ministers from going against an overwhelming majority of the population.

## INTERNATIONAL INTERVENTIONS

There was a time when two great opposing countries, along with important allies, basically ruled the world. They had the biggest armies and the biggest budgets, so they would decide the faith of all. In yesterday's context, it probably couldn't have been any different. Does it still make sense today? Do we really want that for the future?

Even armed with the best honorable intentions, should one country (or just a few countries) have that right? When the interventions are economically and politically motivated, some crises are left unattended. Needy people in unacceptable conditions are left behind. We cannot ask one country to save the world from tyranny and bring peace and democracy to every country in need of help. Its people should not pay the heavy price and suffer the casualties by itself.

*The whole world has to get involved in the name of democracy.* Interventions create enemies. Why should they aim their anger at one country when the rest of the developed countries have the same wish? Wouldn't it be different if the terrorists had the entire planet as sworn enemies?

The Arab Spring has taught us that younger generations in many countries wish for change. What if the United Nations, NATO, G7, the World Bank, and all international political forces consolidated powers to offer different models of democracy to choose from—plus a concrete plan of action?

The population of each country must make the final decision. We certainly do not need some New World Order or an international governing entity. It would only mean more confusion and chaos. We need a common platform of expression for the people to influence the powers in place.

It has to start with a call to action from the people of a country to its leaders. If the government did nothing, the rest of the world would only step in at the demand of a majority of the country's population, represented by the United Nations and all other international institutes. The procedures would be predetermined, and the new democratic system chosen by a consensus of its population would be ready to implement.

The next step would be a serious warning from the world to the dictator in question. The first option is to leave power immediately—and only then would it be possible to ensure his or her safety. In the name of diplomatic avenues versus violence, the population of that country must give its dictator a chance to leave peacefully. What if the dictator could have guaranteed asylum and the assurance that he or she won't be imprisoned or tortured in any way? What if he would be left with enough to maintain an acceptable lifestyle? Wouldn't he or she be more willing to leave? The reward of change is worth the moral question of letting a dictator go with minimal consequence. The price of war is also too great.

If the government did not want to step down, there would be a massive response from countries that were joined for a common mission. The international community would step in with hundreds of thousands of soldiers. The operation would be quick and help would remain to ensure a peaceful transition.

We could apply the same principle for African countries that want the world to intervene. We, as an evolved species, should never allow human suffering of any kind.

We must exercise the same sense of urgency when a natural catastrophic event hits. We forget that humans are part of nature, and catastrophes are as urgent as a tsunami. I cannot imagine a truly evolved society letting horrible things happen to its own people. A common platform would demonstrate that an overwhelming percentage of people agree that humanitarian relief is necessary for all in need. We want to help even if there are no economic or political

**The United Nations and developed countries have the obligation to join forces to eradicate dictatorship and tyranny.**

41

gains. All governments would be pressed to react to a demand made by an important majority of their populations.

The Big Bang Project proposes to take on that role. This common platform for positive change could be the place where surveys and petitions are grouped for the sake of evolution. With large numbers of participants, we can assemble more people (in the millions), than a hundred manifestations could (without leading to violence).

The United Nations and developed countries have the obligation to join forces to eradicate dictatorship and tyranny. Too many victims are left ignored; the consequences are inhumane. If we put enough pressure on our governments, things can change. If we can group our efforts to try to save endangered wildlife, such as polar bears and pandas, can we at the very least ask for the same passion and commitment for endangered humans?

# CHAPTER 5

# CAN GOVERNMENTS PLAY A BETTER ROLE TO IMPROVE ECONOMIES?

The economy of a country depends largely on two major factors: the strength of the private sector and the efforts of our governments. This chapter is about improving the government's role in keeping the economy strong and growing.

The government plays an important part in a country's healthy economy. It provides the right settings. Governments regulate interest rates, keep inflation controlled, and provide the right environment for investing.

The following ideas are meant to improve the government's involvement in the economy. The total budget of any federal government is enormous. People are taxed more and more to pay for past and present mismanagement.

# A NATIONAL DEBT FOR LEGACY?

Dept-to-GDP Ration 10 Year Trend

| Country | 2004 | 2014 |
|---|---|---|
| Japan | 165.5 | 227.2 |
| Greece | 98.6 | 175.1 |
| Italy | 103.9 | 132.6 |
| Portugal | 57.6 | 129.0 |
| Singapore | 98.0 | 105.5 |
| United States | 62.7 | 101.5 |
| Belgium | 94.2 | 101.5 |

Fig. 7 National debt ten-year trend

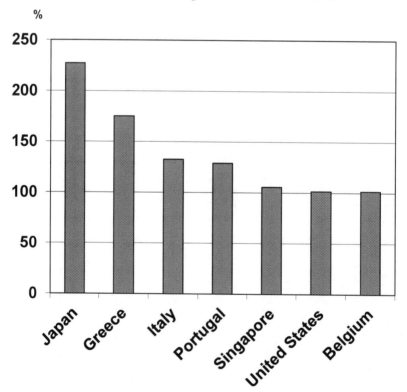

Fig. 8 Debt-to-GDP Ratio, worst situations

The financial situations in most countries are precarious. A balanced budget is not achieved, and national debts increase. The interest portion of the accumulated deficit is more important every year. We are leaving the next generation with an important debt that our own mismanagement created. Is that what they deserve? Shouldn't we have a goal of providing the perfect setting for our children?

It seems evident that a country must be able to pay its expenses and try to generate wealth and an "insurance" reserve to better face future challenges, such as natural catastrophes, difficult economic periods, and long-lasting recessions.

A balanced budget is the base for survival; a positive budget is the base for growth. First, governments must understand basic business principles and the important distinction between expense, interest, investment, cash flow, and leverage.

Cash flow is the difference between money coming in and money going out. Money going out pays for regular ongoing expenses or investments that will benefit generations to come. We invest in infrastructure, schools, hospitals, roads, and bridges. These infrastructures have different life spans. A debt may be generated to support these important investments. The cash flow must be able to pay the interest on the debt created, the portion of capital proportionate to the infrastructure's life spans, and the maintenance required for each.

Debt is created when we do not respect these simple financial principles. Any individual or company adopting the financial strategies of governments would soon be bankrupt.

Leverage is the principle where the positive financial result of an investment is superior to the cost of the debt created. The positive financial stimulus of an investment is supposed to generate income to offset the interest and amortized capital.

It is clear that we are far from creating common wealth for future generations. We are deepening the hole every year. We need to press the reset button and have better financial strategies to improve efficiency and accountability from all levels of governments.

The great target of "Deficit Zero," promised by many politicians, means paying the expenses for the year with the revenues received, without the need for borrowing. That's not enough. It has nothing to do with reducing the debt, which keeps the heavy load of high interest in the government's financial statements.

A country's cash flow must support all long-term investments, pay regular expenses, and reduce debt. Deficit Zero leaves no margin for any contingency reserve for unforeseen needs.

We need to revise every necessary common service. Once we have chosen as a society what we want as shared costs, we need proper management. Departments are presently very badly mismanaged.

Austerity measures proposed by some governments are often disconnected from the best methods for controlling expenses. When some suggest a general cut in all departments of a certain percentage, they are ignorant of the true realities of each ministry. They all must be analyzed individually. Some departments may need higher budgets to better serve citizens, some may need bigger cuts than the average set, and some may need to be completely eliminated. No credible private entity could be managed so blindly and thrive.

Revising total national budgets and adapting the revenues accordingly to ensure that we are able to pay our expenses and investments is a start (a *neutral cash*

**Austerity measures proposed by some governments are often disconnected from the best methods for controlling expenses.**

*flow*). The next necessary step is to accumulate social wealth for future generations (a *positive cash flow*). Until we eliminate the important portion of the debt that should have been paid already, the burden of past mistakes hurts the capacity to grow. Do we know if debts still exist while the lifespan of the infrastructure ends?

Governments must identify and monitor both fixed and variable expenses. Fixed expenses are regular monthly costs. For example, maintenance of a hospital will not vary much every month. Variable expenses will fluctuate depending on the number of people using a service, and the average cost for each service rendered. Companies understand the important distinction between both, and they have tools to identify, monitor, and regulate their performances. Without these crucial financial controls, it's like running blind. The sad fact is that this is what most governments are doing.

## PERFORMANCE INDICATORS

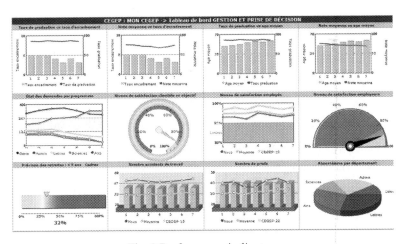

Fig. 9 Performance indicators

Usual economic ratios such as GDP (Gross Domestic Product), inflation rate, unemployment rate, and import/export are important performance indicators. They indicate the strength of the country's economy and wealth.

When we analyze these ratios, we judge the government. Who is really responsible for most of these indicators? The economic trades, which come from the private business sector, make all the difference. Large and small businesses generate wealth for the country by producing jobs, trades, and profit. They pay taxes and reinvest in the economy with new ventures. Governments often take credit (or blame) for these ratios at election time. That's fine, but somewhat irrelevant in most cases. We should be able to monitor the performances that relate solely to the government.

Any serious organization striving for continual improvements must be able to measure and benchmark its performance. These ratios are compared with past performances, the averages of the industry, and the best performers across the world. We all feel there is a lot of waste of efficiency at many levels of government, but it's difficult to quantify without financial ratios. All credible corporations use precise measuring tools to measure performance.

The goals and targets are realistically obtainable, and the task of the government is to provide all the right tools to reach, if not surpass, them. The strategy is to get inspired by the best methods known and apply them while constantly trying to develop better ways.

The following are ratios that would enable the population to better rate the performances of their elected officials. These are to be analyzed deeper, and they should be viewed as a first draft for new ideas to improve our governments. Experts and hobbyists are welcome to comment and submit important ratios that are not listed below. They need to be "personalized" for every department of public expenses.

- ratio management/employees (in number of employed and in dollars)
- number of public workers per service (per thousand people)
- price per mile (or kilometer) for infrastructure (in square feet)
- average cost per habitant for specific services

- average number of services received by recipients
- average delay before every service is received
- average service rendered and cost per person actually using the service
- measure of satisfaction from users
- financial ratios (cash flow debt coverage, capital versus debt, and expenses versus revenues for each department)

We should have periodical follow-ups on the performance ratios we will agree on. These report cards would be the basis of the government's track record. Every quarter, these numbers could be updated. It is important to realize that each improvement relates to important dollar amounts. A 1 percent difference in a few of these ratios could translate into billions of dollars. Again, this is the part that could save us a lot of wasted dollars. If each department had the best possible results, countries would have more and better services for less.

Opinions are subject to interpretations and distract us from the facts, but numbers don't lie. They reveal an exact measure of performance and efficiency. Transparency from the government is key. Numbers may not lie, but politically motivated twits can deter the truth by changing a parameter that will show better results in ratios while no real improvements have been realized. My government has shown us better numbers in waiting times to get health services. When we dig deeper, we realize that they have added a step in the process. Now you get to talk to someone sooner, but that person's role is to dispatch. People are not really treated faster—even though they have been "taken care of" faster. The base for calculating all ratios must be totally transparent so that we keep uniformity and compare apples with apples, so to say.

**Opinions are subject to interpretations and distract us from the facts, but numbers don't lie.**

How often have we heard the leader of a newly elected party give the same excuses when retracting his or her electoral promises? "We didn't really know how bad the budget was managed by the last government. The situation is worse than we thought. Unforeseen poor financial situations make it impossible to honor our promises." Having the right performance indicators would make that speech unnecessary.

## EVALUATE PUBLIC SERVICES AND COST SHARING

I find the present political arguments about public spending completely irrelevant. The endless negotiations about cutting so many millions in expenses on one side and the other side asking to raise revenues in proportion are void of true sense. The politicians are always vague when we ask where they would specifically cut. Shouldn't it be the other way around? Isn't it about making sure the revenues are enough for the services the population chooses to be shared?

What if we started from scratch? Let the people vote on the services the population wants to be considered as shared public expenses. Everyone must know how much every department—and its services—really cost them for their specific tax brackets. A special referendum on public expenses would settle the ongoing dispute of politicians so we can at last talk specifics and see action. The essential thing is to pay the right price for the services we want. Once we choose what we want—and really know the financial implications—the government must simply comply. The task of the government is to make sure that these services are provided with maximum efficiency.

Often, exemptions or special tax credits were given to lobbyists and important political party donors without the population's endorsement. All the promises to special contributors throughout elections in the past are still part of the budget, but do we really want to pay for all of them? Can we really afford them?

These special favors are added to the expenses we all pay for. They have been accumulating with every election for a long time, resulting in important amounts. Companies making extraordinary profits still benefit from unwarranted tax breaks. Why don't we press the reset button and reevaluate who should receive special tax credits—and for what reason.

## EVERY DOLLAR COUNTS

Fig. 10 Large pot, what we don't see.

The total revenues of a country's government represent an extremely large sum of money. It becomes too easy to lose sense of what it means. So many politicians throw statements about cutting a billion here or millions there. When we suggest a cut, the amount is not what we want to hear. We want to know what can be done in what department and how many dollars it will save. You can't cut a service that is said to be public unless the population chooses to stop receiving that specific service. It is not up to politicians to make such a decision. We never hear exactly who would be impacted, or how much, when politicians on all sides argue about how many millions we can take off that large pot of money that the total budget represents. What does a billion dollars really mean in relation to a country's total budget? The numbers are so big, and we have lost track of what they represent.

When dealing with one large budget, the amount is so large that it is easier for corruption to set in. But if we separate the total budget into smaller amounts, it is more difficult to hide behind.

Fig. 11 Budget divided by services

A billion dollars would have more significance if we spoke in the context of a specific service or department. Comparing billions to smaller amounts puts it in a comprehensive context. Each department could be considered as a separate budget, detailing smaller subdepartments, and representing smaller amounts. This way, we can relate better with the larger sums of money and what they mean in terms of their true impact. It also becomes easier to identify waste, mishandling of public funds, and corruption.

Question every expense and determine who it benefits—and who should be responsible. What if we approach every expense by analyzing the beneficiaries and who should be financially responsible? We hear of the *user-payer method*, but it lacks precision. Take an infrastructure like a bridge. You may never cross the bridge, but you still benefit from that bridge because it allows people, merchandise, and supplies to get to your community. The same question applied to every department would reveal that three entities are great beneficiaries: the person receiving the service, society (governments), and industries (representing all relevant fields of the private sector). The next question is what proportion of the total financial responsibility each one should assume.

That line of questioning leads us to another question: How can the responsibilities be best shared? Sometimes sharing cost is not enough or does not reflect the reality about who benefits versus who is responsible. The contributions of each entity could be reevaluated to improve efficiency and fairness.

More importantly, when responsibility is directly linking a specific department to the true beneficiary, efficiency is increased, total cost is diminished, and services are improved. The savings in efficiency could result in lower taxes and a balanced budget.

**Question every expense and determine who it benefits—and who should be responsible.**

Wouldn't it be great to receive a statement of services received from every department and your exact portion of taxes for each? Don't we deserve a detailed invoice like we get from all services received from the private sector?

We see more and more situations where a partnership between the private sector and government is considered, and it is increasingly applied. What if we pursue that concept one step further?

What if we rethink the concept of public/private partnerships? Every department could create the best partnership model to ensure that there would be no waste of money due to overpaying and/or lack of efficiency.

Roads and infrastructures are major investments for society. The huge contracts are often given to the private sector. Only a few companies with the proper equipment and expertise can execute these construction projects. They offer their services to the public sector, and the cheaper offer is often selected. The value is not often questioned. These private companies have created a monopoly in this sector. They make a lot of profit, sometimes using less-than-ethical strategies to increase their profits. The amounts are so important that it has attracted the greediest. Corruption is far too rampant.

Many big players have taken advantage of the present system, including engineering firms, unions, politicians, and suppliers. "Brown envelopes" have been known to circulate. The lack of transparency is evident. Information about key performance ratios is not available to the public. The present system allows such transgressions; this is what we need to change.

What if we created a new type of partnership between the private and public sectors? A private corporation obtaining a government construction contract is likely to have more contracts in the future. A new entity should be formed with a real partnership between both sides. This government can own 45 percent of the new company; private companies own 55 percent. This type of association makes sure that the government is participating in the profits. Instead of only private companies making enormous profits from government jobs, everybody wins. It is okay for a company to make a reasonable profit, but at this moment, it is probably not the case. Equipment may be rented from the private partner at a fair price for the projects. There would be no room for corruption because all the costs and corresponding performance ratios would be provided to the population. Transparency would be required in all projects.

Performance indicators would make it possible to measure the true price paid per mile (or kilometer) and compare it with the average price paid on all public and private industries for similar contracts. The idea for government to partner with the private sector is to save money compared to the cost of executing these projects with only public equipment and employees. If it ends up costing more, we need to revise our ways.

We need to reinvent our present models; a new approach is the only way to stop the bleeding. When the system opens the doors to corruption and exaggeration, pointing fingers at the guilty parties does not solve the core problem: a failed system.

The questions of who benefits and who should be responsible can take different forms of shared responsibility, depending on the department.

Let's take education as example. Shouldn't the proportion and type of responsibilities change with every stage of education? What if we divided education into three major groups? Instead of simply paying into a large generalized budget through our taxes, what if we divided the different costs according to level of contribution from individuals, society, and industry. It would better reflect the principles of shared benefits and responsibility.

## DAY CARE AND KINDERGARTEN

In the preschool stage, the responsibilities should be between the parents and society. The industries do not need to be implicated in that stage of education. Society would provide the infrastructure and administration costs, and the parents would pay an important part of teacher salaries, according to their salary tax brackets, to be determined by the population. People with no children in that age group would pay their parts in infrastructure and administration through taxes, but we need to ask parents for some financial contribution.

Parents are important beneficiaries of preschool services. It must be considered in all fairness. At that crucial stage of development, the presence of a parent is the greatest gift a young child can get. In kindergarten, the child starts to experience life in society. Before that stage, we should ask parents to not exceed a few days per week of day-care service. Great social savings can be made while we give what's best for our young children. An additional tax break could be given for parents who choose to have one parent stay home to care for the baby. Society, parents, and children would benefit from such measures.

Who benefits and who should be responsible offers a fairer way to share the financial accountabilities between individuals, society, and industry. The situation changes in the next phases of education.

## PRIMARY SCHOOL AND HIGH SCHOOL

Society should have most of the financial responsibility in the stages where we prepare our kids for the future. Parents could pay extra for books and supplies—and maybe a part of the transportation costs. The rest could be covered by taxes, which everybody pays. Every developed society must provide education for all children, no matter the social status. A good education for children is the basis for a country's strong future economy.

Each stage of education needs to be analyzed separately to identify who should be accountable. So far, the industries have not been affected much, thus reducing their social responsibility. The importance of the industries' contributions is far more relevant in the next stage of education.

> **Each stage of education needs to be analyzed separately to identify who should be accountable.**

## COLLEGE AND UNIVERSITY

Colleges and universities prepare our grown children for jobs and careers. There is presently an important gap between the reality of the job market and traditional education. Many diplomas are given without any demand in the workforce. And many good jobs find no takers for lack of trained skilled candidates.

Here is where the private sector should step in. The future workforce will be their employees. The better students are prepared for their future jobs, the better the private sector will be able to perform and remain at top competitive level. What if industries took on the major part of the logistics, training, recruiting, and specialized education?

Who is better equipped to teach skills and knowledge needed in today's workforce reality for all the different trades?

The best know-how and training methods in every sector of activity are more important and relevant in the private sector. Each trade and industry has specialized training for its employees. They have the best equipment and facilities. They would recruit according to their specific needs, connected to the strengths, skills, and wishes of youngsters. Education would be tailored to better serve true needs by providing more on-the-job training. Companies know their requirements better than the government does. Right now, we are more reactive than proactive in matching skills with the right jobs. The private sector would most likely have better results.

Some students fail in traditional education because of low grades in courses that have nothing to do with future required skills. Students lose the opportunity to prove themselves where it matters most, and society loses good workers because of a failing grade in history, geography, or philosophy. Being connected to the real world would certainly motivate and encourage a lot of youngsters who are lost in the present education system.

Efficiency and cost control should be optimized by the private sector—instead of the government—to eliminate the widespread lack of efficiency in the public sector.

**Some students fail in traditional education because of low grades in courses that have nothing to do with future required skills.**

College and university infrastructures should be designed according to different industry specifications, and society should pay an important share of infrastructure and maintenance costs. Different industries should supply equipment, teachers, and trainers. The industries already have state-of-the-art technology. They could integrate these facilities to complement colleges and universities.

For higher education, university students have responsibility since they will benefit from better salaries and conditions. Society needs all trades. Is it fair to ask youngsters who have pursued professional careers such as plumbing to pay the part of the student who goes further—while he or she is already contributing with his or her share of taxes for society? Future university graduates will have better-paying jobs; shouldn't they also be financially responsible? Financing at no interest must be available for the less fortunate—either from industries and/or the government. No one should be refused. Society needs the top students to go as far as possible. The future elite must not waste any great young minds.

What about other departments? Why don't we consider this line of reasoning for all the different ministries? Health care is an important cost for every society. Again, let's look at who benefits and who should be responsible. Individuals, society, the medical and pharmaceutical industries, and insurance companies are all important players. Let's see how it can play out.

Most developed countries are still trying to find a better way to handle expensive health-care costs. When the public sector takes care of it all, you find longer waiting lists and poor efficiency, driving the budget very high. Some countries provide a very good public system, but is it costing too much? My country's health-care ministry's management structure is so complicated that no one can really understand it, but we all know it's inefficient. Again, performance indicators would answer these questions.

With private insurance companies, the coverage needed is often too expensive, and too many people cannot afford it. Many do not have access to health care. How can a developed country leave some of its population without the possibility of receiving care?

The following is an alternative for countries without a public health-care system. It may even prove to be more cost efficient than most public health-care systems.

A small percentage of people are responsible for a large portion of total health costs. Since not everybody is insured in some countries, the price for coverage is very high and supports a few very costly patients. What if we divide in the following manner?

## SHARED COSTS FOR PEOPLE WITH SPECIAL HEALTH-CARE NEEDS

Those with special chronic health conditions or accident victims are not equipped to pay the astronomical costs of long-term special care. They represent a small percentage of the population—but the most important part of total national health-care costs. Their private health insurance is too expensive—or they are not accepted for insurance coverage. As an evolved, developed civilization, we need to take total responsibility in the form of a shared cost through our taxes for all people in such health situations. These unfortunate people could be you or a loved one. The need to get the care they need, and doctors and specialists could invoice the government. Of course, the services provided would be charged at a reasonable regular price. Detailed statements would be available to the population (as should every private company providing products or services to the government). Ratios can and will be compared with other countries and the private sector.

## PRIVATE INSURANCE FOR SURGERY—MORE PERSONAL RESPONSIBILITY FOR REGULAR CARE

There has to be personal responsibility for one's health. If we are ready to spend hundreds for our cars when they need repairs, why not pay for personal care to reduce everyone's taxes? Private insurance combined with a minimum amount covered by the government (to be determined by the population) would represent a fair system. Insurance would need to be a little more expensive for smokers, overweight people, and those with self-inflicted conditions.

Those who are in great health—whose healthy lifestyles keep them away from hospitals—deserve to be compensated with less expensive personal insurance. Governments should pay for the pregnancy and birth process.

In order to ensure that the goal of a fair system is respected, those who refuse personal insurance will still get health services when needed, but they would be invoiced the total cost, plus a small, but fair, penalty. They penalize people who are insured in the sense that their premiums would be lower if everybody was insured. Governments could finance with low interest rates. This would encourage everyone to get insurance to avoid the risk. People on welfare who cannot afford insurance or services would be taken care of. Society and industry could share the costs.

We need to encourage personal accountability. At least one member of every family should take basic first-aid courses. The price of the courses would be tax deductible. There would be a discount in health insurance and increased security for loved ones, which are good motivations to act.

Many people abuse the system when it's entirely public. They go to the emergency room for a self-treatable, not really urgent, condition. A moderator ticket (service fee to be decided by voters) would reduce traffic, waiting times, and social costs.

The government's responsibility is to provide the hospital infrastructure, a website, and a phone line to inform users about in-home treatments. Checkups and basic care should be at least partly responsible by individuals, which would reduce greatly the total social cost of health care.

By asking who benefits and who should be responsible, we can reduce overall social costs while providing better care. The fact that chronic expensive needs are covered reduces the cost per capita. The insurance coverage would be lowered significantly by only taking responsibility for special needs, such as surgeries and emergencies. Add some personal accountability, and we would have the best system for the best price.

This line of reasoning must be applied to all public services. We need leaders to have open minds to new approaches. Efficiency and fairness can certainly be better respected; this has become a great problem in most countries.

Most countries cannot continue with their current health-care systems. People are still not receiving proper care, and the cost of health care cannot be sustained in most developed countries.

With your feedback, we will find a way to improve the present situation. Our responsibility as individuals is to exercise our rights and exert pressure for change. Peaceful arguments that represent a consensus among the population will make governments consider new ideas.

The next chapter will present ideas to better spread wealth, questioning capitalism and its core problems. Concrete solutions will be presented. We will also see how individual behaviors can transform the way we do business. Companies react to the demand, and they will certainly adjust if the demand forces changes.

# CHAPTER 6

# CAPITALISM: IS THE RIGHT ON THE RIGHT COURSE?

To create wealth, capitalism is the only model. It has many different forms; even communist countries such as China have benefited from this system, which is tailored to enrich society, the government, and a small percentage of individuals. We have witnessed the great rise of the Chinese impact in the world's economy thanks to trade and a unique version of social capitalism.

The original concept of capitalism gives the opportunity to individuals to improve their financial conditions by starting and operating businesses. Instead of having concentrated wealth limited to a few, anyone who has a vision and the drive to make it happen can do so. Unlike any other economic system, the social wealth grows with every business success, and the creators of jobs are rewarded with financial gain. People may achieve a luxurious lifestyle if they persevere and work hard.

Thanks to this system, great business achievements changed the world. Incredible fortunes were created, and a lot of people benefitted in many different ways. Innovation is a constant: finding better ways and better products, and remaining competitive by continual improvements. These are the advantages that everyone benefits from in some way.

In theory, the more wealth that is created, the more people benefit. The social net should be improved and better service should be provided to society. But in practice, the "losers" of this system are left in poverty. Some people do not even have access to the essentials and basic care that any evolved society should make available to all its citizens.

Social inequality is getting worse and worse. Unemployment is increasing in many parts of the world. Quality jobs are rarer, and the middle class suffers. With a gradually diminishing disposable income, while being solicited more and more, it seems the situation has gotten worse for most in the past few decades. What happened? Is there a solution to reverse the trend?

## THE GAME CHANGED, BUT WHO HAS THE ADVANTAGE?

Capitalism has evolved immensely since it began. The parameters are very different from a few decades ago. Opportunities for start-ups have become very rare compared to my father's generation and his father's. It is the result of capitalism natural evolution. In the beginning, entrepreneurs owned companies and grew them. Gradually, the expansion of these businesses and the fight for market share became the norm.

Big players kept growing at a very fast pace. Mergers, acquisitions, and geographic growth eliminated most of the smaller players. Local businesses cannot compete against huge companies that offer cheaper prices and more choices. Volume gave them special conditions with their suppliers; most paid lower salaries or exported production to save even more. They constantly increased their market shares, killing more and more of the smaller businesses.

The cycle of regional poverty continued to grow, and the middle class was gradually dragged into precarious financial situations. As small businesses tried to save themselves from bankruptcy, they had to lay off people and/or lower their hours. Many small companies ended up not surviving, leaving people out of work. These people worked harder in worse conditions—lower salaries, part-time schedules, and no benefits—for bigger companies. With a limited disposable income, people were forced to buy from the big companies because of the savings offered, but they still found it difficult to make ends meet. The social costs of unemployment grew, and we asked the victims to pay the bills.

Banks do not want risk, and it becomes increasingly difficult to find financing when you want to start your own business. Only the big players have the best borrowing rates and conditions. The opportunity gap grows bigger between small and large companies. The wealth is concentrated in huge headquarters, benefitting fewer individuals. Market shares are dominated by the big international entities and they are the best prepared to take the rest. That trend is unlikely to stop unless there is a profound change.

We need to find better ways to generate and spread wealth.

## TOO BIG TO FAIL EQUALS TOO BIG TO EXIST AS IS?

When entities are called "too big to fail," it means they have become too big to be efficient. The concentrations of profit and risk are too important. If they fail, the repercussions are important for more than the company alone. The result may be catastrophic for the entire community.

When they do well, the wealth is concentrated in a very few. Their influence becomes too important for one entity. They control markets, making it impossible for small and medium businesses to compete.

**The opportunity gap grows bigger between small and large companies.**

When "in the name of profit" has important negative consequences for a lot of people and society, there's a serious problem.

In the name of profit" gives the big investors, such as banks and investment firms, the power to create trends in the market, based on speculation tactics and volume. It has become comparable to a casino. The bank always wins.

Investing is no longer a question about the company or its vision, mission, and strategies for growth. Today, most investors have a short-term strategy. They are more preoccupied by the trend of the shares. The actual details of companies they invest in are no longer important for day traders. I once asked a specialist in day trading the following questions. "Do day traders know, before they invest, the competitive edge, the challenges, and the opportunities of the companies in their market, the strengths, and weaknesses?" The answer was no. Have they made a complete "PESTEL" analysis (political, economic, social, technological, environmental, and legal) to understand the trade? He answered again no. Have they analyzed the contingency plans of the company for possible challenges? The answer was of course not. They look at the curb of the share value on a micro scale. The fluctuations within hours, minutes, and seconds will be the basis of their trade decisions. It's all about the trend of the shares—and nothing about the company. Small investors and companies may become victims of such strategies.

Can you imagine a company's management team, before going public, questioning its share value every hour and every minute to see how much the company is worth? Do you think a crisis in the Middle East is new for a company that has been in business for years? Do they panic every time it happens? Why does it make sense that the company's management should be concerned about daily fluctuations once it joins the stock exchange? How does it become relevant all of sudden?

Imagine a company being faced by devaluation because its shares suffered an unjustified drop and investors panicked. Big movements in shares are the bread and butter of banks, big investment companies, and day traders. No one has the magical crystal ball when it comes to accurately predicting the future values of shares. When an investment entity is big enough, it has the power to create trends and influence the market. Is it really helping companies and the economy? Who really benefits from these investment speculation strategies?

When you invest in a business project, such as a restaurant, retail store, manufacturing, or real estate, you create jobs. You build a long-term economic driver. You need builders, suppliers, and office works. You create a positive economic impact in your region.

Investors with long-term vision, like Warren Buffet, will invest in an industry that has been analyzed deeply for short- and long-term potential. These investors make a positive difference in the economy by helping promising companies to grow.

What if we revise the cycle of investments on the open market? What if we could buy or sell shares only every quarter (three months)? The nonsense of daily fluctuations, which only benefit a few "too big to fail" organizations, would be greatly reduced. Every quarter, a window of time—two weeks or so—may be given for market adjustments. To keep stock exchanges running, different industries could have different cycles. After that predetermined period, people could buy or sell, but the stock value would not change until the next quarter. In the interim, investors would be welcome to look for private, regional business opportunities.

Some, if not most, that are described as "too big to fail," abuse that position of strength and adopt questionable ethical behaviors to their advantage. Whether it is the power of lobbying, political donations, misleading investments, or industrial spying, it seems they'll do whatever it takes to feed the growing appetite of their shareowners. They have been known to copy patents; since no one has the financial resources to beat them in court, they don't even bother trying. They can buy you out and kill your idea because they see it as more of a threat than an opportunity. They understand that being too big to fail means they can bend the rules.

There are some benefits to having large entities. They have huge budgets for research and development and they can undertake projects that no small companies could.

Aren't there ways to achieve these goals with alternative ways? The big question is how we want, as a society, the wealth to be distributed. The larger entities continue to grow at a pace no one else can match. The billionaires enrich their fortunes exponentially faster than the less fortunate; the gap is increasing at a quicker pace every year. Do we want wealth to be accessible to as many people possible?

To encourage growth and wealth is great, but how much is enough? Do you need hundreds of millions of dollars to be happy? Is greed so strong that you want more—even when you make more in one year than hundreds could ever spend in their lifetimes? Do you prefer a lottery where you have one chance in a billion for a billion or a chance in a thousand for a million? Aren't a thousand millionaires better than one billionaire?

The ultimate evolution of capitalism in its present form will lead us to a few individuals controlling everything, which is a frightening similarity to a dictatorship. Is that what was originally intended when this system was created?

## THE RIGHT'S SOCIAL RESPONSIBILITIES

The pressure from investors to constantly increase profits leads to decisions that do not serve anybody else but them. When short-term profit is privileged, consequences happen. Disregard for environment and social issues, is the norm—all in the name of profit.

The pressure exerted by environmentalists on the polluting industries was enough to

**The idea is that capitalism must understand and honor its social responsibilities, including environment, employment, and higher education.**

convince governments and companies to react. The population's general awareness and concern also makes a big difference. There is still a lot of work to be done in that regard.

A new generation of leaders is becoming more concerned about environmental issues; there is even a Master of Environment Management (MEM) offered with MBA (Master of Business Administration) programs in many universities. This important challenge is being addressed for the future way of doing business. That's encouraging.

The idea is that capitalism must understand and honor its social responsibilities, including environment, employment, and higher education (as proposed earlier).

## AVOID THE VOID; THERE ARE NO JOBS THERE.

Fig. 12 Falling into the jobless void

When the Right proclaims that the solution is a smaller government, who becomes responsible for people in need? They create unemployment by exporting production where it is cheaper so they can make more profit. Who should be responsible?

Governments sometimes choose austerity measures and cut jobs because of budgets—instead of asking how the service will be affected. The real questions should be about the true repercussions of the cuts. The strategy for all governments should be to encourage growth and maximize efficiency in all public services.

With aggressive austerity measures, we are left with more and more people in the "void." The void is that empty space between group A and group B. Group A is the jobs provided by the public sector and group B is the jobs provided by the private sector.

That void has grown bigger, and once you're in it, it's very difficult to get out. The victims lose their jobs and have to pay more with fewer contributors.

Setting the right conditions to favor the best social leverage, added value, and maximum employment is the role of government and industry.

Fig. 13 Unemployment, source Business Insider

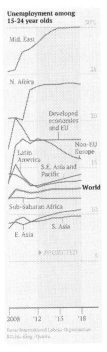

Fig. 14 Youth unemployment forecast

## WHO BENEFITS THE MOST WITHOUT THE RESPONSIBILITY?

What if the social cost and responsibility of the void could be shared by the industries? They created it after all.

What if companies were obligated to find other jobs for the employees they intend to cut or replace? What if they had to provide proper training for new careers and pay an important part of unemployment costs until new jobs are found?

What if companies were penalized for having a certain percentage of employees overseas by paying additional taxes? Wouldn't that be fairer? Maybe, but more can be done if we create an advantage for the bigger entities to spread the opportunity of business growth—and not to spread their fortune. Money is spent quickly, but business projects create jobs and grow wealth.

Also, our war veterans deserve to have the Right and Left team up to make sure they are not left in the void after serving their country. Even if we are against war, soldiers merit our true admiration for their ultimate sacrifice. They should be first in line for jobs in the police force, fire department, and security positions in the public and private sectors.

## EVOLVING FROM "WIN-WIN" TO "WIN-WIN-WIN"

The next step is to include some social issues on the list of industry responsibilities. A win-win scenario is when a transaction or partnership offer advantages for both parties. We need to add a third party to the equation: society.

The approach proposed in the previous chapter of analyzing who benefits and who should be responsible still applies to the quest of finding better ways. Considering environmental, economical, and other social impacts should be the basis of future business making.

What if there were incentives for companies to produce more locally? Isn't there a possibility to offset some of the social costs and encourage profitability for all?

Can't we invent a win-win-win situation? Large entities can profit, and so can business partners and society.

The alternative is worst for the Right. If we continue with no changes, we will reach the point where the system is most likely going to fail. Its failure will happen when people stop believing in their chances. The "losers" of capitalism will be left with no—or very little—social help. Many people will live in poverty and lack the basic essentials. The population will opt for a socialist system.

If the corporate world does not provide a better social net than a socialist system would, why create wealth if it's reserved for only a few? What's the advantage for the overwhelming majority of poor people who live in worse conditions than they would in a socialist or communist country that at least provides health and education for all? If the best solution for the population is to be content with an average lower-middle-class lifestyle and forget about the American dream because it's out of reach, it will be the greatest failure of capitalism. The ideology will have lost all credibility. The infamous 1 percent now possesses close to half of the world's wealth. This dangerous trend is worsening every year; is that success for capitalism?

If the Right does not react quickly, the worst-case scenario for its own future may happen sooner than anticipated. People who have no hope of getting out of poverty will feel discouraged and desperate. Corporate giants need to ask themselves how far they have stretched the elastic—and understand that it's just about to break. The status quo is not acceptable; even the winners of capitalism may be in financial danger if the system fails.

# CHAPTER 7

# CAN CAPITALISM BE SAVED?

## RETHINKING OUR BEHAVIORS

Capitalism is based on the great balance between offers and demands. Offers have the power to influence demand, and demand can influence offers. Our buying behaviors have an important impact on local economies. Every purchase we make has social repercussions; being aware is the first step.

We are partly responsible for the course capitalism took. Offers created a demand based on price and we responded by looking at our own wallets. How can we ask for change if we don't adapt our shopping habits?

## THE GREAT COST OF SAVINGS

Let me share an all-too-common scenario, illustrated simplistically. The not-so-fictional town was once called Happy-Ville. The names are fictional; any resemblance is unintended and should be taken as coincidence.

Fig. 15 Welcome to Happy-Ville

Once upon a time, a beautiful town called Happy-Ville was thriving. Local businesses were healthy, and entrepreneurship was everywhere. Bob, the local butcher, and Jane lived on the same street as the local mechanic (Jim) and Jill, the local hardware store owners (Mike and Nancy), and a local shoe store partner (Henry). They were all friends and met often.

The population was growing, and bigger chain stores appeared gradually. Large retail surfaces with head offices elsewhere—who sold products made overseas at much cheaper prices—gave the population more buying power. Thanks to the great savings available, it became easier to "keep up with the Joneses."

One evening, Dave, who just moved in town for a good job at Buzco, invited the street neighbors for a barbecue. Everybody was having a great time, but it turned awkward when Dave started showing off. He was proud to flash his huge new barbecue and lawnmower that he got at great prices at the new Big House Hardware store.

Dave's brother started bragging about the great deals he got at another new store called Buzco. He showed the steaks and burgers he bought there for the barbecue, and he was proud to state the price differences compared to the local butcher, without realizing that Bob was seated right next to him.

Henry inadvertently heard Jane talk to Jill about the great discounts on shoes she saw at Allmerd and told her how she encouraged her friends at the office to go there to check it out—and that she should do the same.

The malaise grew deeper at every following party. No one was serving beef from Bob the butcher, no one was wearing shoes from Henry's store, and no hardware from Mike's hardware store was to be found in the neighborhood. Jim had not seen any of his friends at his garage because his prices were slightly above the new competitor, Buzco.

Gatherings became fewer—and then gradually quite rare.

A few years later, Bob had to close shop after the bank foreclosed on his house. Jim sold his home at a loss and moved to an apartment building, which was owned by Mr. Swung (the son of a rich Chinese manufacturer). Bob lived with his two kids, one floor above Mike and Henry's apartment. He got a job at Big House Hardware at minimum wage. Mike and Henry were unemployed and shared a small apartment. They did occasional maintenance work for Mr. Swung—who owned many apartment buildings—to help pay the bills.

Bob still met his old friends often, but not at parties and barbecues. Instead, they saw each other at the apartment, Allmerd, or Buzco, looking for great deals.

There were clothing and bicycle manufacturers in town, but they both closed. Their customers had owned shops in surrounding cities, but most of them closed. They tried to sell their products to Allmerd, but they were turned down because of prices and production volume capacity.

Teens had no jobs, and graffiti was everywhere—even on the Happy-Ville city sign.

Fig. 16 Graffiti on town sign

## BUYING IS VOTING

The most important message the Big Bang Project is trying to convey is that every action we decide to take has an enormous impact. Individual contributions can change the world, which was demonstrated in the second chapter. We can make an important difference if we get more involved in the democratic process.

Environmentalists awakened us by making us aware that every time we waste or pollute, we contribute to our own demise. We are learning to reduce, reuse, and recycle. We are learning that respecting our planet is respecting ourselves.

**Are the savings really worth encouraging local poverty?**

Growing awareness has already made an impact in the way we all behave. Politicians and business leaders are adapting—slowly and gradually—to include environmental issues in their decisions and challenges.

Social responsibility affects every purchase we make. Before you buy something, consider the local economic impact. Are the savings really worth encouraging local poverty?

Should we say bravo when you show how much you saved on your online purchase or at a chain store? Maybe we should we ask three simple questions that make all the difference:

- Where do the resources and materials come from?
- Where is it transformed and assembled—and where are the jobs created?
- Where do the profits and applicable sales taxes go?

Who benefits from your purchase? What's the contribution to the local economy? These are crucial questions. Is it better to have many cheap T-shirts made elsewhere or a few quality T-shirts made locally? Is it better to shop online—saving local and national sales tax—and killing local retail stores? The economic repercussions are added to the environmental impact of increased pollution from individual home deliveries. Is it the smarter choice?

The social price we all pay for buying based simply on price is great. You don't get personalized service, and the quality is often questionable. We weaken the economy, kill local entrepreneurship, sacrifice good jobs in the manufacturing sector, and help pollute our planet. Is it really worth it just to save a few dollars?

**Your voting power is expressed every time you make a purchase.**

Buying is voting. Your voting power is expressed every time you make a purchase. Think of the number of votes we all make every day.

It's not once every four years; it is hundreds of purchases every month. That's voting power.

Individual actions, repeated by a large number of people, can reverse the trend. It all depends on us. Are we willing to change our consuming habits? Will we continue to think selfishly when we buy and not care about the social repercussions? Your future votes (purchases) will tell.

## CAN LABELS CHANGE YOUR VOTE?

Fig. 17 Local economy check

What if we identify products that promote the local economy? We already have ingredient labels. We also can see if something is kosher or from organic farming (without chemicals). Shouldn't products that have an important percentage of local economic repercussion be identified? A simple label showing where the resources came from, where the jobs of transforming the product came from, and where the head office is can help people make the right choices.

What if products identified with a "local economy check" are exempt from any sales taxes? What if products that score zero in the three questions proposed above had an additional tax to compensate the negative local economic impact?

Many products are imported because they cannot be produced locally, and this is normal. For example, production of coffee and bananas cannot happen in all countries. In these cases, that component must be excluded from the local economy label ratings.

## THE BEST MODELS FOR SPREADING WEALTH

The challenge is to encourage entrepreneurship on a local and national scale. If we give privileges to business models that spread wealth, important changes may happen. What if large companies had everything to gain by adopting better business models?

Business models that share wealth better than others already exist. The idea is to encourage these economically healthier models.

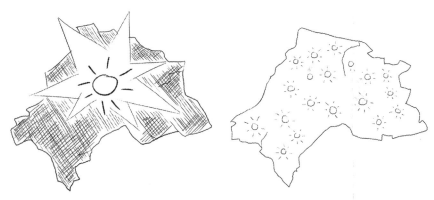

Fig. 18 Spreading wealth, the choice is clear.

The year of cooperatives was 2013. This business model is still not exploited enough. A co-op may be used for many different projects— from community urban gardening projects to regional and national banks. Unified membership and partnership can take a variety of arrangements for its associates. The goal of a co-op is not to generate maximum profit but to benefit from its fruits in different manners, such as local contributions, group savings, other logistic advantages, autonomy, and growth by reinvesting in the organization and the community.

Franchising is also a great model for partnership that promotes shared responsibility and wealth. A centralized office provides notoriety, expertise, financial incentives, and operational know-how. Responsibility for local operations is given to franchisees. They own their company, and sometimes a partnership is made with the franchisor. The franchisee pays an initial franchise fee and monthly royalties to the franchisor, but the profit belongs to the franchisee, a local entrepreneur. This formula is great for expansion. Business partners who finance the central banner's growth make local investments. It's a true win-win-win business model. The head office grows, businesses remain local, and a significant proportion of taxes on profits stay in the community.

Entities that are centralized are less adaptive, offering little flexibility for local demands; it's all about mass production. We must all conform to maximize their profitability. There is a total disconnect to regional reality.

A global centralized operation is vulnerable to recessions and volatility, but local markets are easier to predict and adapt. Some markets thrive in certain regions, and other regions are in recession. A centralized operation may need to shut down, sacrificing many jobs, while a franchise system may close a few locations, but it is still able to keep the better ones alive and growing.

At the same time, a region is vulnerable when it relies on only a few industries. How often have we seen a town that relies on one industry shut down as soon as the manufacturer shuts down? That one industry supported all other businesses in town, selling its products and services to the workers. The impact becomes so great that the town becomes a ghost town in no time.

The choice for continued growth is to aim for fair profits for the maximum number of people instead of maximum profits for a few. Fair profit also means less volatility. Every product has a different radius to obtain a fair and steady profit. It all depends on the demand of every region for every product.

The goal is to bring production as close to the consumer as possible, for as many products as possible, while being profitable enough. Bringing production closer to the market allows other competitive advantages and distinctive skills that mass production cannot offer. "Just-in-time" deliveries and the possibility of ordering frequently in lower quantities helps increase stock turnover and reduce risk, which increases profitability. Service is also much better when you are closer to your customers, sharing the same time zone and language. Better quality products are a competitive skill that you cannot provide with mass production at the cheapest possible cost.

Governments should create incentives for large centralized companies to adopt a formula inspired by partnership models that spread local entrepreneurship while growing with minimum investment.

Investors, large and small, may partner with local entrepreneurs and operators. Through regional chambers of commerce, they could choose to buy a regional partnership in a franchise or other type of association. Local companies and large centralized companies, private or public, may present business plans to the chambers of commerce in different regions. It is increasingly difficult for small companies to obtain financing at banks. A new approach for financing local companies would encourage regional growth. These investments make a difference in the economy—much more than speculative investments from day trading and short-term investing, which benefit from market volatility instead of stability and honest growth.

Municipal and federal governments may provide incentives for all parties that invest locally. Any start-up needs help in the beginning. Creating the right conditions to help companies "too big to fail" to regionalize operations can certainly help make a difference. Many forms of government assistance may be used, such as exemptions from municipal taxes, tax credits on regional investment, and no penalties if investments come from different retirement tax shelter funds. Companies selling franchises to regional entrepreneurs should have a break on capital gains taxes. If any combination of these incentives were put in place, growth would easily offset the tax exemptions offered. Reviving regional economies is the greatest investment we can make; the repercussions will last a long time.

The tax breaks could be progressive, lasting from three to five years. This social investment will create long-term revenues far exceeding the initial costs, which is the best possible scenario for maximum leverage.

There is a distinction between encouraging regional growth and protectionism. In fact, regions should not be economically separated by "borders" but rather with an economic elasticity.

Free international markets are vital for strengthening local markets around the world. There is a subtle, important nuance between aiming for independence and striving for regional autonomy. True independence means that one requires no help or intervention by anyone on the outside. Autonomy is a goal where everyone in every region is serving their community and contributes to help other communities—just as other communities may help them.

When a developed country comes to the aid of a country in need, the goal is to provide the tools, training, and know-how so they become self-sufficient one day. Simply giving money does not have the same positive results, especially for long-term and continual growth. Autonomy can only be achieved with the help of others.

As suggested in a previous chapter, the Right must take responsibility in social issues that benefit itself as well. Everybody wins when the service provided is better, at lower costs. The Right would significantly lower taxation rates by taking on responsibility for social needs, such as higher education and job creation, through local entrepreneurial partnerships.

# TECHNOLOGY AND SERVICE

Technology has enabled us to massively produce using machines instead of humans. We also invented ways to destroy the planet. Does this mean we should use them? When machines replace workers in the name of profit for one organization, is technology really serving society by eliminating more jobs?

Technology's role is to improve our global situation. How and for what we use it is the crucial challenge. If its goal is to create full and productive employment—and then improve efficiency and job quality—the true objectives of technology will be reached. If it is used to better the situations for a few, with negative consequences affecting many, technology will have failed its true mission.

# CHAPTER 8

# THE BIG BANG PROJECT'S REVIEW AND ACTION PLAN

Positive evolution for mankind rests in our hands. Let's review the ideas of positive realignment proposed in the first phase of the Big Bang Project.

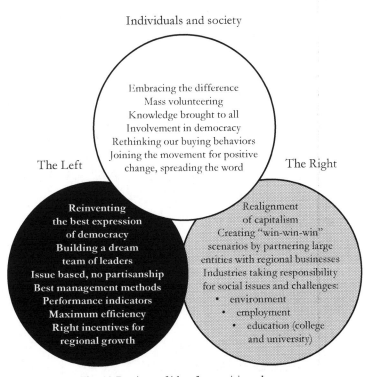

Individuals and society

Embracing the difference
Mass volunteering
Knowledge brought to all
Involvement in democracy
Rethinking our buying behaviors
Joining the movement for positive
change, spreading the word

The Left

The Right

Reinventing
the best expression
of democracy
Building a dream
team of leaders
Issue based, no partisanship
Best management methods
Performance indicators
Maximum efficiency
Right incentives for
regional growth

Realignment
of capitalism
Creating "win-win-win"
scenarios by partnering large
entities with regional businesses
Industries taking responsibility
for social issues and challenges:
• environment
• employment
• education (college
and university)

Fig. 19 Review of idea for positive change

We have demonstrated that individuals and society can influence change. Governments and corporations, formed by individuals to serve society, have to join the efforts of transformation. In periods of important transitions, the challenge for all is to adapt, as Darwin so brilliantly proved in the theory of evolution.

The Right, the Left, and society are closely intertwined; the relationship among these three groups must be aligned with the same mission. The common denominator of these great forces is us. If we, as individuals and as a species, decide to focus our efforts on resolving global challenges, we will strive. Action by all is required to make sure positive changes happen. The day every human has the right to a decent life, live his or her passions, contribute to society, access to education, and aspire to better his or her conditions is sadly too far away. The day when all will be respected by all will be a glorious day for mankind; let's make it reality.

Striving for a better world means that we must create the perfect environment to strengthen every social core. Individuals, families, communities, and regions make a country strong. A strong country provides the best opportunity for its citizens. Our task is to make everyone shine to the fullest; we all stand to gain.

## The common denominator of these great forces is us.

Let this book be a conversation piece. What fun it can be to reinvent the world around the dinner table with friends. Talk about it, share ideas, and participate in this era of positive change.

Your feedback and involvement will help create the best path for positive evolution. This first step toward mankind's positive evolution is only the beginning of many more steps to follow.

This book is the first phase toward reaching our goals. It is supported by a website so we can have your feedback, ideas, inspirations, and questions. You will be able to learn more about great causes that you might want to get involved with.

My ultimate goal is to find better ways for the evolution of mankind. It is not about being right on every subject. I will be truly honored by any constructive feedback—even if you disagree with my ideas. I am curious about your arguments and other solutions you propose. Analyzing all the options will help us get closer to the best answers.

I will consider my plan a success only if you are one of many to embark in the Big Bang Project's ambitious dream.

## THE BIG BANG PROJECT'S ACTION PLAN (PHASE 1)

1. Read this book, react, and spread the word—by any peaceful means you see fit—so the maximum number of people participates in this new conversation of positive change. Register if you represent an organization of good so those who wish to make a difference can be inspired to join your cause and help. All organizations—large and small—are welcome, as long as there are no exclusions based on faith, gender, sexual orientation, political conviction, or social status.

2. Go to www.thebigbangproject.com to see how you can find your personal way to contribute. New organizations will join regularly. Visit often.

3. Just do it. Get involved. Join an organization that suits you best for the cause. Learn how, when, and where you can help. You can also take part in the discussions about changes proposed for the Left and Right.

4. Prepare the next phase. Gather the results, input, and ideas that represent a true consensus on measures to initiate.

5.  Use the Big Bang Project's powerful, unified influence to change things. This is not a revolt; it is a presentation of concrete ideas in a peaceful manner that politicians and industry leaders will have no choice but to listen to and adjust accordingly.

6.  Participate on an ongoing basis.

Everything is in constant movement and evolution; this great cosmic law is demonstrated in nature. We need to continually question ourselves, reset, refocus, and react. I don't see the day where all will be perfect. Changes are gradual and take time, and many issues need our attention and follow-up for many years to come.

Evolution is determined by actions and events, not by time. We can certainly speed things up with the addition of more and more people getting more and more involved.

I have a great trust in the younger generations to be open to change. The older generations have a responsibility to help them mold a future that belongs to them. I propose a New Year's resolution for mankind: mobilization for positive change. Let the Big Bang Project be the start of a new, shared vision.

I can't wait to get your feedback. Without it, the next phase will never happen. I will compile and analyze all comments and answers from the first phase. New questions will be presented, new points of view will be discussed, and better answers will be proposed.

I ask the media to help spread the news and make the Big Bang Project known to all. Only the media can make that happen. Their involvement could make the difference in the success of this great plan. Paying attention to positive news is what people need for a change.

# CHAPTER 9

# RELIGION—SADLY, AN IMPORTANT ISSUE

We all agree that religion—although a very sensitive subject for many—must be addressed when analyzing humanity's evolution. A valiant effort must be made by everyone to wear the Humble Human hat.

How we have handled differences in religions and faiths has been the source of more discord than politics and other social issues. Let's all take a step back and determine the true purpose of religion and its true goal. Should it be a personal spiritual quest or a social, cultural, and political issue?

We are at a critical point regarding religion. The original message has been distorted over many centuries. War and divisions are all we experience today, instead of achieving its goal of inspiring human wisdom, spirituality, connecting with our inner essence, universal cosmic consciousness, understanding our roles in life, motivating for peace, respecting creation, and embracing diversity.

The result after hundreds of years is war, which has created deep divisions. We must

> How we have handled differences in religions and faiths has been the source of more discord than politics and other social issues.

conclude that the mission of religion has failed. We all have been exposed for so long to religion; it is almost ingrained in our DNA. This explains why our beliefs are so strong. A form of collective brainwashing that has lasted for centuries made it extremely difficult to break free. Some are victims of extreme brainwashing from radical groups, resulting in perpetual conflicts.

The evolution of mankind depends largely on the evolution of spirituality. Again, how we approach the question of religion has driven us to deep, unjustified divisions. When trying something for almost two thousand years—to mostly negative results—any evolved species would try a new approach.

Asking everyone to become atheists or subscribe to the same religion in the exact same way and interpretation is unrealistic and completely disconnected from nature, "cosmic" common sense, and true spirituality.

We are all unique. We come from different cultures and beliefs. Everyone sharing a religion is unique in the way he or she experiences spirituality. Each human has a personal relationship with God or his or her gods. We must understand, respect, and embrace that.

This beautiful diversity is seen everywhere in nature—and even in space. Isn't it normal to expect there is a dimension where spirits exist? These energies with consciousness are as diversified and have none of the physical limitations humans do. To presume that God is omnipotent, and that his species exists only as one supreme unique entity, is against the most basic law of nature and cosmic common sense.

Isn't it normal to assume that God or gods would try to communicate throughout history to different cultures by using different cultural references, languages, and images? The names of messiahs and their interpretations would logically be adapted to be understood by a species in a somewhat "infant" stage of development. If the Messiah chose to show up 2,000 years later, would his speech be the same? What race or religion would the Messiah choose if he decided to come back? Representing one religion would be a bad strategy. He would have no credibility with other faiths and cultures. How is it possible to communicate to all? The answer is to change strategy and be present in everyone's essence with a personalized communication, using references that speak to each individual. The message of respect and peace can be delivered in many ways.

The truth is within us, and communication must happen from our inner souls. The answers you need are personal. The spiritual answers are distinctive for each; our questions and realities are all different. God communicates directly with you through your soul—not through any third party like religion, offering general spiritual interpretations. Each soul is unique and needs personalized communication with God.

We all have an inner sense of right and wrong; religion is optional. Our values and actions reflect what we truly believe—not our choice of "messenger." Do you need to believe in Santa Claus to be a person who loves to give? The essence of giving is more important than the image used to represent it. The same applies to religion.

Religions have been in a standstill for more than a millennium, but all other aspects have evolved tremendously. The gap between evolution in science and societies versus religious beliefs is bigger than ever. Religions were created when the world was completely different. We once thought gods were responsible for rain and earthquakes, and all natural wonders were considered miracles. The way to expand was to conquer, which is irrelevant today.

> We all have an inner sense of right and wrong; religion is optional.

We must remind ourselves that previous generations wrote spiritual texts with their cultural reality and limited understanding of the world and the universe. Are they really the absolute reference?

Since the beginning of time, trying to understand the grand cosmic truth has been a major quest for humans. Spiritual leaders exist in most cultures—from ancient African and Indian tribes to the most modern of societies. In every corner of the world, people share a fascination for the unknown. Philosophers, prophets, visionaries, and scientists are still trying to explain mysteries.

Now that science has invalidated most of the religious notions regarding the creation of the universe, the sun, the planet, and humans, can we evolve our spirituality toward true wisdom and real peace?

Most currently influential cultures have evolved over the course of the previous two thousand years, but should religion question itself seriously to reflect the reality of today's world? So many different faiths share the world; multiculturalism was unheard of when today's religions began taking popular hold. For example, when Christianity was popularly believed to be a minor cult, Romans massacred Christians for sport in the coliseum. Then, after some time, Christianity was declared the official religion of the Roman Empire. It goes to show the changing of tides. Human establishments, like organized religion, fluctuate with popular opinion while spirituality, on the other hand, simply persists. Can today's religions change their point of view?

Culturally evolved cultures understand that there are no subcultures and that women deserve all the same rights as men. These societies have benefitted greatly by respecting every human being, encouraging every member of society to learn and contribute to society. Women have proven they can be great leaders and contributors; everybody wins by including them in decision-making roles. Can religions catch up?

Now that a vast majority of people on earth understands that homosexuality is not a crime or a disease, the real crime is to impose and force anything on anyone. Consenting adults expressing their sexuality are far more acceptable than the behaviors of many (even within churches) who use authority to abuse woman and children. The offenders are still welcome in church. Can't religions evolve too?

## THE GREAT PLAN FOR PEACE

The best possible scenario to get us closer to peace is that we focus on shared values by all religious groups. We need to understand the distinction between culture, politics, and spirituality. The big question is not who or what you believe in but rather what you do with it and how it is expressed through your actions.

The first step is to offer a platform of expression for all moderate people of all different faiths. We must reunite in peace and find common ground. We must demonstrate that an important majority of every religious group respects and embraces spiritual diversity. We must consider it a strength—not a weakness. The Big Bang Project's website offers a place to reunite people from all different backgrounds and religions toward a common goal of peace. The arguments of peace coming in great numbers, from all angles, can help potential and existing religious extremists see reason. The results may also inspire religious leaders to update their own vision of religion and spirituality.

We need all Muslims to be on the front line in the fight against terrorism, the Twitter hashtag "#NotInMyName" is a great start. Join the conversation in great numbers and show the world that your faith is totally against what extremists stand for. Remember how you were welcomed in democratic countries. Muslims live in peace on all continents with neighbors of different faiths; they can practice their religion in peace. That's something to fight about.

## THE SUMMIT OF ALL SUMMITS

The next step is to reunite all religious leaders, from all credible faiths, and write a joint letter of peace to the world.

The leaders must take this opportunity to become proactive to change. This would be the summit of all summits. Imagine all religious leaders in the same room, shaking hands and crafting a peace resolution among all religions.

This symbolic agreement can change the world. I call upon religious leaders to be the inspiration for wisdom. Put an end to the unjustified violence in the name of God. Imagine being remembered by your historical legacy of peace for mankind.

If we extract cultural differences and focus on the basic message of spirituality—instead of who delivered it—we will find that all religions have much in common. That's the mandate our religious leaders have.

Here's a suggestion for a draft for a much needed religious peace resolution:

We, religious leaders, hereby declare peace between all faiths. The following is a consensus of shared values among all religions:

- We are all united by the belief in a greater, superior, nonphysical consciousness.
- All religions are at the service of people—not the other way around.
- Our role is to accompany, guide, and inspire people on their spiritual journeys.
- We offer a great diversity of images and words, delivered by different messengers to assist people to connect with inner spirituality.
- We respect and embrace all cultural and religious differences.
- All religions condemn any violent behavior, verbal and physical, in the name of any god or religion.
- It is strictly forbidden to impose a faith on a child, woman, or anybody with different beliefs. Everyone is welcome to believe—or not—in any religion.

- All religions encourage helping one another—regardless of faith.
- All religions serve the same cause: peace in your soul, and on earth.

All religions must join to eradicate all form of violence. Humanity's evolution went from being able to kill larger, stronger, and faster animals from a distance to being able to kill more and more humans. Is it evolution or devolution? Can religion help humanity understand the right path of evolution and help mankind evolve in peace?

Fig. 19 Religion equals peace?

Fig. 20 From evolution to devolution

When you really think about it, there is an ultimate, undisputable conclusion about the afterlife.

First, we must all recognize that we are still very ignorant about the afterlife. The proof is that we have no irrefutable proof that has convinced everybody without any doubt. Faith has divided people in different beliefs and we are still fighting after hundreds of years. We argue about a subject that even religious leaders can't really answer with certitude. Science is still far from explaining everything about the reality of "the other dimension." Those who have lived near-death experiences only stayed a short moment and they observed a small part of that world, a kind of vestibule. The best psychics cannot answer all questions: How is a soul born? Does it need energy to sustain life? Does it die? Are we eternal? How far and how fast can a spirit travel in the universe? Have our souls lived in beings other than humans? Who really goes to heaven or hell? Why?

**First, we must all recognize that we are still very ignorant about the afterlife.**

We place much importance on this matter because it pertains to our future. The thought of eternal life may be comforting, but it still is the greatest unknown. Let's take a step back and try to approach the question with logic and common sense.

Three possibilities exist:

- When our bodies die, we stop existing. Our spirits die with our bodies.
- Spirits live without bodies, but there is no judgment, hell, or heaven. Spirits simply unite with other spirits of their choice.
- Heaven exists. We will all be judged before having access to paradise.

If we assume there is a greater power in heaven, we have to logically assume that this entity is much wiser and smarter than humans. This means that he will not blame you for who or what you believe in. He understands that your religion, culture, family, and friends have influenced you since childhood. He will forgive you for your ignorance. He really has no human name; names were given to him in so many versions, using so many images throughout history. How can the "Prime Grand Consciousness" have a name when there were no parents?

God or the gods will instead judge your actions in life. You will need to answer the grand questions: What have you done with your faith? If you were blessed with any gift—power, fame, or wealth—what did you do with it? Were you a positive energy or a negative force in the human world? Did you do the best you could to spread kindness, love, and understanding?

Regardless of your faith, God knows—or the gods know—that it is irrelevant, considering all the influences everybody has been exposed to. He is obviously more evolved than humanity, and he must judge with fair rules.

No matter how it turns out in the afterlife, the certitude is that we have been fighting for nothing. Even worse, we are insulting the Creator by disrespecting his creation.

God is more evolved than humans are. He is not egocentric, selfish, or greedy for fame and power (like we are). A "creator" does not need to be worshiped. He only wants us to respect, worship, and cherish all of his creation: all humans, our planet, and everything on it. Any parent can relate. The day your baby is born, it is no longer about you. It is all about your child. To kill and destroy ourselves is the greatest tragedy for the "Creator of Life."

Peace on earth is God's only true wish; our survival and evolution can only happen if we understand and respect his true request.

## LETTER FROM HUMANITY TO RELIGIOUS EXTREMISTS

A noble cause must be served by noble actions. Your actions are contrary to the message of your own religion. Your actions have taken away all credibility to your cause. You are seen and perceived as being completely brainwashed, having lost reason and the connection with your inner sense of right and wrong. How can a human being commit such horrific acts in the name of any God? Have you no heart? No religion teaches to fuel hatred with revenge or creating tactics of fear.

**He only wants us to respect, worship, and cherish all of his creation: all humans, our planet, and everything on it.**

You definitely got our attention, but in the worst possible way. Instead of being sympathetic to your cause, your choice of inhumane violence versus the choice of arguments has rallied the whole world against you.

A rare world consensus: You have gone way too far. No reason can justify such unthinkable horrible acts of violence.

You represent a very small minority even within your own faith. Your world representation is therefore insignificant. Your army may be quite impressive, but it is no match compared to the combined world armies. Your true odds of winning are nil.

The world has evolved greatly while your beliefs remained in a standstill for centuries. Your barbaric ways belong to an era long gone. Your interpretation of religion is disconnected from today's reality. It belongs to a time where some faiths believed the world was flat and if you traveled to the edges, you would fall in hell. And the list of misinformation from all religions goes on. Do you honestly believe that physical rewards are waiting for you in heaven, such as virgins, good wine, and a feast? How can you expect a nonphysical dimension to provide physical gifts? Questioning ourselves to continually improve is the basis of evolution. Science and culture have moved forward; why can't you?

Hell must be overcrowded. According to you, everyone who does not believe in your god is going to hell. Think about it, have all the civilizations throughout mankind's history that existed before your religion was created gone to hell simply because they were never introduced to your god?

All of humanity with different faiths—even societies that ignore the existence of your god—are going to hell? Any person with great values who spreads love and respect while being a positive contributor to society deserves to go to hell because his or her spirituality is expressed differently than your religion? Only a seriously brainwashed person can really believe such nonsense.

How many generations must pay for mistakes of the past? We agree that many behaviors of imperialism have been wrong and unethical throughout history. The great powers colonized continents with no regard for what they considered subcultures.

Must we punish present generations for all the errors of our ancestors? This logic suggests that we kill all Germans, including newborns, because of what Hitler did. All Americans should be tortured for the days of slavery? All descendants of all civilizations that conquered should still be punished? How far back must we go? How long will this last?

The world needs to move on and look toward the future—not relive the past forever. This eternal grudge and need for revenge serves no positive purpose. You must get out of this unending loop of violence, which only leads to self-destruction.

Who is the greater man: the one who believes women are his possession or the man who understands that it is a privilege to be loved?

Who is the better man: the one who imposes his way, the one who justifies his superiority with his interpretation of texts written more than a thousand years ago, or the one who is open for change and encourages all people, especially his loved ones, to speak their minds?

Who is more powerful: the man who keeps women in ignorance to keep his superiority or the man who helps women learn and grow, recognizing women as equals?

Who is the stronger man: the one who forces a woman to hide under a veil because of a barbaric incapacity to see a woman without sexual thoughts or the man who can contain himself and lets women wear what pleases them without having to pay for men's weaknesses? *You are the problem—not women.* By the way, have you tried wearing a burka for a week?

Who is really loved: the man who uses fear and physical violence to maintain control and his superiority or the man whose strength is used to protect—while remaining humble before his woman—and tries constantly to offer her the best conditions for growth with unconditional love and respect?

Would you give the same speech if you were a woman? Haven't you heard the cries of mothers giving birth to girls, knowing too well their fates? Are you that insensitive? Have you no compassion?

Society is the greatest beneficiary of the emancipation, freedom, and equality of women. Women strive and are contributing to the strength of families and communities. We can learn much from their wisdom and sensible perspectives.

Which society is wiser: a culture that persecutes, captures, tortures, and kills foreigners, fellow citizens, brothers, and sisters for thinking differently or societies that have welcomed every race, culture, and faith, building a country based on respect for all? Which countries have offered accommodations to all religions?

Your barbaric actions are not worthy of your religion and are completely inhumane. In the name of your god, in the name of humanity, stop this senseless violence. This avenue will lead to your demise. Democracy is the way mankind has chosen for its evolution. Drop your weapons, and join the conversation toward compromise. It is the only way to avoid your destruction. Choosing the world as enemy is not a good idea.

Only through an approved democratic process may you dream of having a religious state. Any other methods will make your dream impossible. A state that is not recognized by the international community has no chance to survive.

If you refuse to opt for the democratic solution, it leaves you with only one viable option: drop your weapons, surrender, and plea for "prolonged insanity" due to extreme religious brainwashing. Maybe you'll find some clemency.

If you are remotely intelligent, you will understand that pursuing your strategy of violence will only strengthen the international community, which will rally more and more against you. This will result in your death, and many collateral victims will suffer. This is not very smart.

# CONCLUSION

We, the people, can influence human evolution. We have demonstrated in this work that there is no magic solution for a better world. The proposed approach of analyzing the behaviors of the great forces of influence, individuals, society, the Right, and the Left offers a path toward constructive conversations.

With new ideas, change is possible. With the contribution of everyone, as small as it may be, it all becomes probable. Becoming a positive social contributor should be a goal we all share.

The objective of offering opportunities for all is an achievement we can certainly aim for. It is easy to unite when we reach a true consensus for positive change that benefits all. There are ways to reinvent our methods to ensure that there are no losers; together we can resolve our many challenges. As a group, there is practically no limit to our potential.

Simply by respecting and embracing our differences, we can advance to a higher state of evolution. Your individuality is precious, and so is everyone else's. We complement one another with our diversity.

The Big Bang Project is about creating a platform where new ideas are exchanged with respect. Supported by the website, it becomes a call to action. Everyone from different backgrounds, cultures, and faiths is invited to join this movement of positive evolution for mankind.

There are examples where humans show how they are capable of putting differences aside and serving a greater cause. The International Space Center projects prove that countries with divergent political beliefs and agendas can join together to take part in worldly missions. Even though there may be political tension, scientists disregard them and continue to work together. This project is too ambitious for one country to undertake alone. We must join forces for a cause bigger than any country or continent. Let's use this example to inspire humanity to undertake massive humanitarian projects.

Thank you for believing in mankind, for being willing to change, and for being part of the solution.

# TRUE DIRECTIONS
*An affiliate of Tarcher Books*

## OUR MISSION

Tarcher's mission has always been to publish books
that contain great ideas. Why? Because:

## GREAT LIVES BEGIN WITH GREAT IDEAS

At Tarcher, we recognize that many talented authors, speakers,
educators, and thought-leaders share this mission and deserve to be
published – many more than Tarcher can reasonably publish ourselves.
True Directions is ideal for authors and books that increase awareness,
raise consciousness, and inspire others to live their ideals and passions.

Like Tarcher, True Directions books are designed to do three things:
inspire, inform, and motivate.

Thus, True Directions is an ideal way for these important voices to
bring their messages of hope, healing, and help to the world.

Every book published by True Directions– whether it is non-fiction, memoir,
novel, poetry or children's book – continues Tarcher's mission to publish works
that bring positive change in the world. We invite you to join our mission.

For more information, see the True Directions website:
www.iUniverse.com/TrueDirections/SignUp

Be a part of Tarcher's community to bring positive change in this world!
See exclusive author videos, discover new and exciting books, learn about
upcoming events, connect with author blogs and websites, and more!
www.tarcherbooks.com

# TRUE DIRECTIONS
AN AFFILIATE OF TARCHER BOOKS

Printed in the United States
By Bookmasters